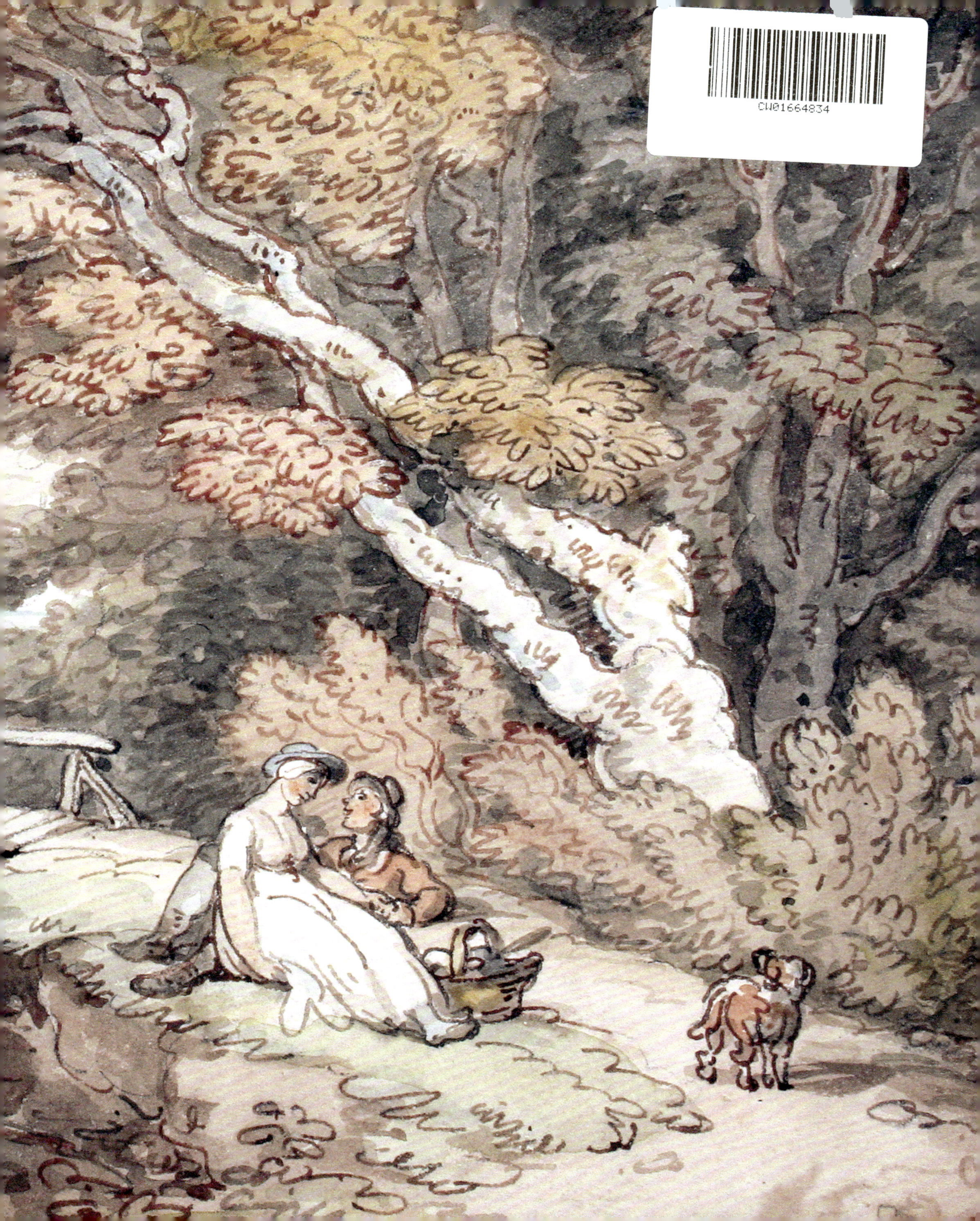

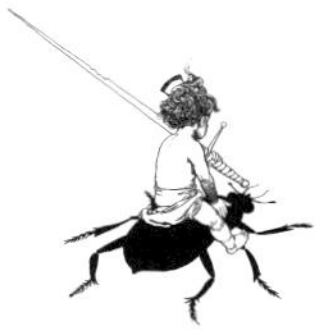


8 & 10 Ryder Street
St James's
London
SW1Y 6QB
020 7839 7551
gallery@chrisbeetles.com
www.chrisbeetles.com

ISBN 978-1-905738-48-9

Catalogue in publication data is available from the British Library

Researched by Eleanor Hall and David Wootton
Written by David Wootton, with notes by Eleanor Hall
Edited by David Wootton
Designed by Jeremy Brook of Graphic Ideas
Photography by Julian Huxley-Parlour
Reproduction by www.cast2create.com
Colour separation and printing by Geoff Neal Litho

Front cover: *A Plate of Oysters* [11]
Front endpaper: *A Sylvan Idyll* [08]
Back endpaper: *Unloading the Shipping* [12]
Back cover: *Beauty and the Beast* [51]

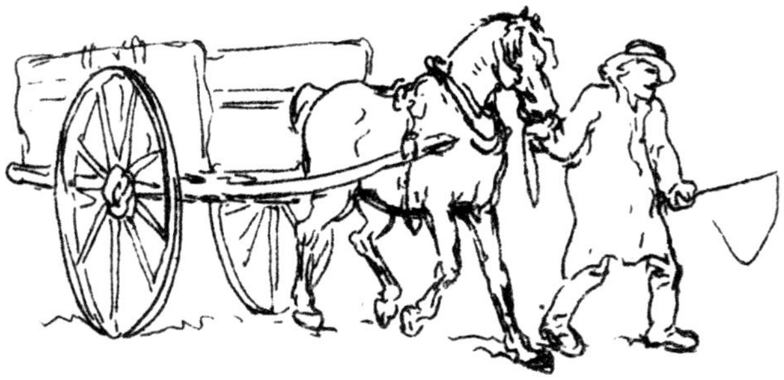

# Thomas Rowlandson

1756/57-1827

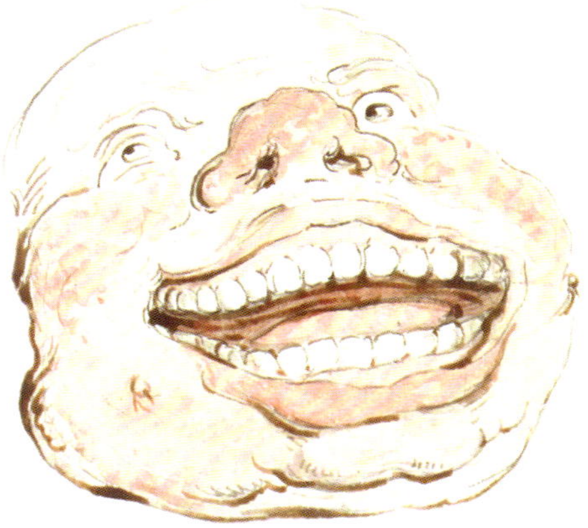

Chris Beetles Gallery

# Rowlandson's Human Comedy

It may come as a surprise to find that Thomas Rowlandson was the exact contemporary of William Blake (1757-1827). Probably the two finest figurative draughtsmen working in London at the turn from the eighteenth to the nineteenth centuries, they both spent time training at the Royal Academy Schools, and both developed as printmakers and illustrators. Yet they are rarely if ever mentioned in the same breath, and indeed seem to have inhabited different cities, if not different worlds. If Blake was preoccupied by the vertical pull between Heaven and Hell, then Rowlandson focussed on the horizontal and, more at ease with his surroundings, provided the public with an essentially secular panorama of the human comedy. Though famous as a social caricaturist, able to define familiar types, he had extraordinary thematic range and technical confidence, and could handle the bawdiest subjects with delicacy of effect.

**Caricature and Idealisation**

Rowlandson's earliest drawings date from his time as a student at the Royal Academy Schools, during the period 1772 to 1778. They were produced almost exclusively in pen and ink over pencil, with one or two including shading in grey wash. Both in atmosphere and technique, they reveal the influence of John Hamilton Mortimer (1740-1779), whose work Rowlandson admired and owned. John Hayes believes that 'it was Mortimer's restless romantic imagination, interest in caricature and the macabre, and vigorous draughtsmanship that most deeply affected Rowlandson's early style' (Hayes 2004, page 13). However, his early exhibits at the Royal Academy, between 1778 and 1781, reveal a gentler, more easily pleasing aspect, comprising for the most part small watercolour portraits of attractive young women drawn in the manner of Francis Wheatley (1747-1801) and John Raphael Smith (1752-1812). While this contrast between two modes – of caricature and idealisation – provided the foundation for his art, the young Rowlandson ensured that he broadened his artistic horizons: by studying sculpture (at the Duke of Richmond's gallery), travelling abroad (to France) and collecting engravings (including some by Rubens and Hogarth).

**Matter and Manner**

In the 1780s, Rowlandson developed his skill as a caricaturist, and especially his ability to exaggerate facial features. By so doing, he showed awareness of the images of Pier Leone Ghezzi (1674-1755), which, in their engraved form, provided a British audience with a shortcut to the Italian caricature tradition. Rowlandson himself may actually have encountered Ghezzi's work in Italy, for there is some evidence that the English artist was in Rome in 1782, though by that time he was already providing caricatures to London publishers and printsellers, notably Hannah Humphrey (active 1778-1822), who was closely associated with Rowlandson's friend and fellow artist, James Gillray (1756-1815). While rarely so savage a political satirist as Gillray, Rowlandson soon gained a reputation as 'the ingenious *Caricaturist*' (*Morning Herald*, 25 December 1784, quoted by Hayes 2004, page14).

Yet caricature was but one of Rowlandson's gifts. During the early 1780s, his compositions gained in elegance, by drawing on the French Rococo, while his landscapes increased in lyricism, by emulating those of Thomas Gainsborough (1727-1788). John Hayes looks to one work in particular as a sign of this growing sophistication: *La Place des Victoires* (private collection), a view of Paris, produced in 1783, on his return journey from Rome:

> *now he began to use watercolour to supplement the wash, what the eighteenth century called a tinted drawing, at the same time developing his subject matter into a more elaborate kind of narrative, replete with interrelated incident, and combining caricature with an elegant figure style.* (Hayes 2004, page14)

Across the remainder of the decade and into the next, Rowlandson tested and extended this maturing style during a series of sketching tours, both at home and abroad. The first native tour, to the Isle of Wight, was possibly inspired by the picturesque theories of the Rev William Gilpin (1724-1804), and yielded 69 drawings in 12 days. Rowlandson made them in the company of his close friend, Henry Wigstead (died 1800), who would publish accounts of two of their subsequent trips: *An Excursion to Brighthelmstone made in the year 1789* – a destination now better known as Brighton – and *Remarks on a Tour to North and South Wales in the year 1797.*

In the present catalogue, these tours are represented by drawings of the West Country and Yorkshire, as well as Wales. Cornwall proved a particular and regular draw as, from the mid 1790s, he was invited to stay with the banker Matthew Michell (died 1819), the first of his two major patrons, who owned the estate of Hengar, north of Bodmin. The Devon town of Okehampton was on the direct route from London to Cornwall and, with its picturesque castle and priory ruins, it provided an attractive stopping place for an artist [14, 15]. Then, while staying at Hengar, Rowlandson made 'countless drawings of the Cornish countryside, which are among [his] most lyrical works' (Hayes 1972, page 20), including studies of some of the more remote corners of its coastline [13]. Michell also joined him on one of his most important foreign trips of the period, that to the Low Countries and northern Germany, made in the early 1790s.

Included here is a characteristic sample of Rowlandson's countless sketches and studies, which together testify to how little evaded this artist's eye or hand. There is an example of the kind of transport that he himself may have travelled in, a Paris diligence [38], which was cheap and roomy (according to Edward Planta's 1816 guidebook, *A New Picture of Paris*). But he was aware of all forms of conveyance from the most rudimentary sedan chair [31] to impressive masted cargo ships [22]. From the window of his carriage or the saddle of his horse, he surveyed his fellow men both in crowds and as individuals. They come together to buy and sell [24], to build and harvest [26, 29], and possibly to beg and borrow, if not steal [32].

The speed with which Rowlandson must have worked ensured that the immediacy of his sketches was retained in his finished compositions. So the very pen line used to depict a treasured moment between a soldier and his girl implies that his inevitable departure is imminent [06]. And when the figures are presented as particularly static – as with pairs of lovers in a wood [08] or a family by a country road [07] – the setting often provides a contrasting dynamic quality, with branches stretching across the space, and foliage apparently rustling in the breeze. Then where the focus is on individual figures, the physique and physiognomy tend to be emphatic and mobile. There is, for instance, no mistaking the chemistry between the man and the woman in *The Alchemy of Love* [04] or the extreme appetites of the diner to the right of the group in *A Plate of Oysters* [11]. The 'interrelated' nature of Rowlandson's narratives, highlighted by John Hayes, is at work not only between incidents within an image, but between the matter and the manner.

**Prints and Illustrations**

In 1798, Rowlandson began to work for his second major patron, Rudolph Ackermann (1764-1834) of the Repository of Arts, at 101 Strand. Over a period of two decades, he provided Ackermann with some of his best drawings for publication both as prints and book illustrations, Ackermann capitalising on developments in colour reproduction. An early example of their collaboration was *Cries of London* (1799), to which Rowlandson contributed 'Characteristic Sketches of the Lower Orders', a visual typology paralleling the lyrical typology of the cries themselves. So the Plant Seller sings 'all a-growing, all a-growing' as he lifts a shrub from his cart, the contents of which appear to present a Rowlandson landscape in miniature [10]. Like many of Ackermann's enterprises, it consists of a theme and variations, while suggesting the thoroughness of contemporary encyclopaedic projects.

Among the most frequently praised of the collaborations between Rowlandson and Ackermann are *The Microcosm of London* (1808-10) and *The Three Tours of Doctor Syntax* (1812, 1820 and 1821), each comprising three volumes. *The Microcosm* was intended to inform both inhabitants and visitors of the rich variety afforded by the capital, and did so in earnest; originally issued in 26 parts, it has 100 illustrations jointly worked by Rowlandson and the architectural draughtsman, Augustus Pugin (1768/69-1832), and accompanying texts by William Henry Pyne (1770-1843) and, for the final volume, William Combe (1742-1823).



By way of contrast, *The Three Tours of Doctor Syntax* was satirical in purpose. It originated in 'The Schoolmaster's Tour', a series of plates by Rowlandson, accompanied by William Combe's verse narrative, which appeared in Ackermann's *Poetical Magazine* in 1809-11. This lampooned the Rev William Gilpin's phenomenally influential writings on the Picturesque, and in turn proved highly successful. Its success lay, in part, in Rowlandson's thorough understanding and more than partial acceptance of Gilpin's theories, which encouraged artists and their audiences to use a set of predefined aesthetic principles to articulate their experience of geography. At the end of the work, this British counterpart to Don Quixote returns home from his wanderings, only to be confronted by his wife, complaining that 'You have not writ your boasted book; Yes, all your money you have spent' [50].

The success of Doctor Syntax led Ackermann to propose a further subject to Rowlandson and Combe, that of 'The English Dance of Death', an original take on a trope that had been popular in Western visual culture since at least the fifteenth century, and for which Hans Holbein the Younger had perhaps provided the standard, with his woodcuts of the 1520s. Again, the 'Dance of Death' suggests the possibility of a theme and (almost unlimited) variations: the personification of mortality visiting representations of different kinds of humanity. Its application to an English context provided

Rowlandson with a structure for his diverse depictions of native society, and its morals and manners. So *The Coquette* shows a fashionable young woman at her dressing table surprised to find that it is the gentlemanly figure of Death who she most immediately attracts [67]. The 72 prints of *The English Dance of Death* gradually appeared between 1814 and 1816, three being published each month. *The English Dance of Life* then followed as a more cheerful sequel.

Throughout this period, Rowlandson worked with a range of publishers and print-sellers, most notably, from 1806, with Thomas Tegg (1776-1846) of 111 Cheapside. Operating at the opposite end of the market from Ackermann, Tegg issued cheap versions of books no longer in copyright, such as *Baron Munchausen* [49], and sold remaindered volumes at a discount, as well as generating a range of his own publications, from 'extended pamphlets' to 'multi-volume editions' (James J Barnes and Patience P Barnes, in *Oxford Dictionary of National Biography*, 2004, Volume 54, page 27).

Significant among Tegg's output was *The Caricature Magazine*, which 'consisted of five volumes of nearly 500 prints published annually between 1807 and 1812', the prints themselves often being well drawn – by those including George Murgatroyd Woodward (1760-1809), as well as Rowlandson – but 'crudely produced and coloured' (Richard Godfrey, *English Caricature. 1620 to the Present*, London: Victoria and Albert Museum, 1984, page 96). A characteristically robust example of Rowlandson's contributions to these volumes is *Sea Stores*, in which women are likened to goods and chattels to be bought by a sailor at his convenience [55]. If the physical contrast of the white prostitute and her black companion should seem offensive, it is as nothing to the imagery of *Land Stores*, the print's pendant, in which a spindly soldier attempts to 'board' an enormous Afro-Caribbean.

As publishers of the time often blurred the boundaries between individual prints and book illustrations, so Rowlandson elided the various aspects of his output. His experience as an illustrator of novels by, say, Henry Fielding, informed his approach to other subjects as expressed in independent compositions, and so helped him to develop a highly distinct and all-encompassing viewpoint that has led to the coining of such phrases as 'Rowlandson's England'. And, in small ways too, he signaled his allegiance to a literary sensibility – Augustan rather than Romantic – as when he added quotations to his drawings, including those by John Gay [37], James Hook [35] and Samuel Johnson [29].

### Tradition and Observation

Even if only a couple of drawings can be securely dated to his very last years, Rowlandson certainly sustained his output into the final decade of his life. He did this, in part, by adapting or even repeating compositions, sometimes by tracing them [59, 63]. Nevertheless, he continued to work with invention and energy, and stretch himself through study, copying from the antique during a final trip to Italy (after 1820) and returning to his researches into comparative anatomy (after 1822).

Indeed, one of the hallmarks of Rowlandson's oeuvre is the way that it so often holds in balance the lessons that he learned from an – often classical – artistic tradition and the observations that he made out in the world. So 'the virtuous chambermaid', escaping the clutches of her lascivious master [52], echoes the reaction of Susannah to the advances of the elders, as copied from an – as yet unidentified – old master painting [65]. And even the unabashed eroticism of *The Parson and the Milkmaids* [54] retains something of the charming primitive innocence of *A Satyr and his Family Amongst Vines* [64], as based on a design by the sixteenth-century German printmaker, Sebald Beham. Rowlandson met the world on its own terms – confronting even its most savage urges – but transformed it into something more appealing and life enhancing.

**David Wootton**

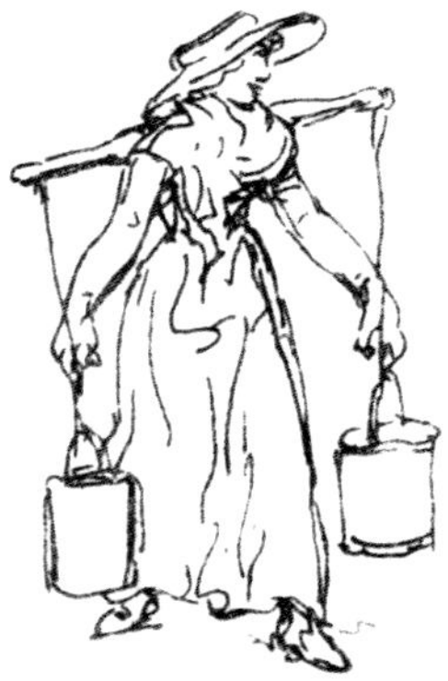

# Thomas Rowlandson 1756/57-1827

**Thomas Rowlandson raised comic art to a new level by representing the panorama of contemporary life with almost unparalleled fluency – adopting lyricism or incisiveness as best fitted the subject. And, in capturing an abundance of picturesque detail, his work provided a parallel to the novels of Henry Fielding or Laurence Sterne.**

Thomas Rowlandson was born in Old Jewry, in the City of London, on 14 July, either in 1756 or 1757, to a merchant in wool and silk. In consequence of the bankruptcy of his father, he and his younger sister, Elizabeth, went to live with their uncle, James, and aunt, Jane, a prosperous Spitalfields silk weaver and his French wife. Following the death of his uncle in 1764, he moved to 4 Church Street (now Romilly Street) Soho with his widowed aunt, and attended the Soho Academy.

From the age of 16, Rowlandson studied art at the Royal Academy Schools, Somerset House, and received permission to draw at the Duke of Richmond's sculpture gallery in Whitehall. Between 1775 and 1787, he exhibited both subject pictures and caricatures, in pen and wash, at the Royal Academy, winning a silver medal in 1777, and making his name seven years later with the ambitious *Vauxhall Gardens* (V&A). During this period, he began to make trips to the Continent (particularly Paris) and in Britain (often accompanied by Henry Wigstead).

Rowlandson continued to live in apartments in Soho with his aunt, until her death in 1789: at 103 Wardour Street (by 1777) and then 50 Poland Street (by 1787). On her death, he received a substantial legacy, though it seems likely that he lost it through gambling. Certainly, through the 1790s, he lived in modest, even shabby, addresses in and around the Strand, finally settling in attic rooms at 1 James Street, Adelphi, in 1800, where he lived for the rest of his life.

Throughout the 1780s, Rowlandson had been engaged in political and social caricature, but his versatility enabled him to work extensively as a book illustrator, initially on the novels of Tobias Smollett and Henry Fielding (1791-1805), and later on volumes dependent on their visual content. Employed by the publisher Rudolph Ackermann from 1798, he depicted the *Miseries of Human Life* (1808) and added figures to Augustus Charles Pugin's architectural settings in *The Microcosm of London* (1808-10). He received the ideal commission in 1812 when asked to collaborate with William Combe, a writer, on *The Three Tours of Dr Syntax* (1812-21). A seasoned traveller, with an extensive knowledge of Britain and the Continent, Rowlandson was well qualified to parody the vagaries of the Picturesque landscape artist. He frequently produced drawings after the Old Masters, and his own landscape style was an adaptation of that of Thomas Gainsborough. During the 1820s, the work of the Italian Renaissance artist, Giovanni della Porta, inspired him to return to caricature, the art that had made his name, and produced a number of comparative anatomy studies.

Rowlandson became seriously ill in 1825 and died at home on 21 April 1827.

The executor and sole legatee of his will was Betsey Winter, his longstanding companion.

His work is represented in numerous public collections, including the British Museum, the National Maritime Museum, Tate and the V&A; the Ashmolean Museum (Oxford), the Fitzwilliam Museum (Cambridge), Hertford Museum, Manchester Art Gallery, the Museum of Island History (Newport, Isle of Wight), Tyne & Wear Museums, Wakefield Art Gallery and York Art Gallery; and Yale Center for British Art (New Haven).

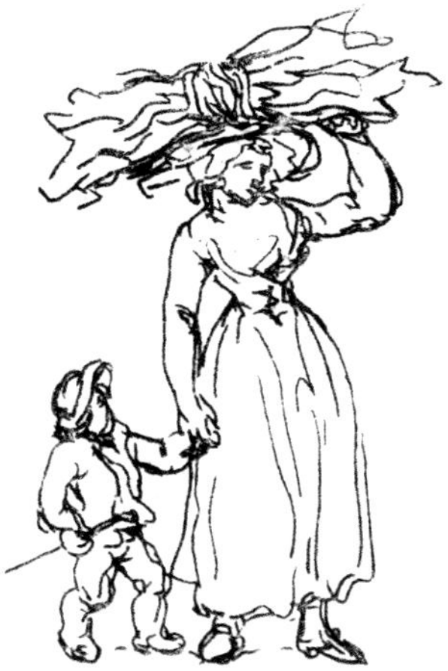

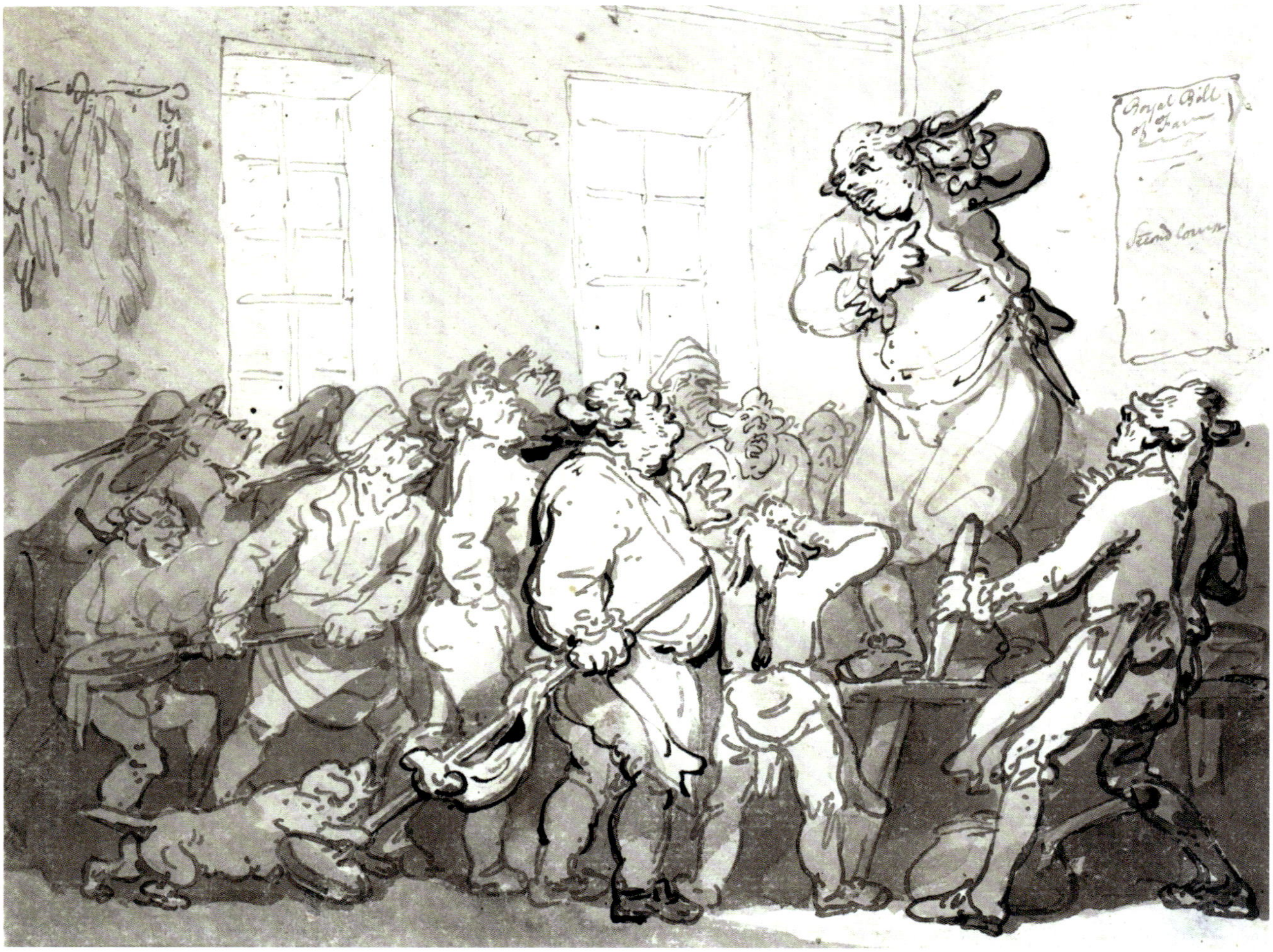



**01** FIERCE AS STARING AJAX, FROM HIS SEAT
UPROSE WITH VISAGE STERN, THE KING OF MEAT

*pen ink and monochrome watercolour*
*6 ¼ x 8 inches*

Provenance: Bernard Houthakker
Illustrated: Peter Pindar, *The Lousiad*, London: G Kearsley, 1786-87, frontispiece
Literature: Joseph Grego, *Rowlandson The Caricaturist*, London: Chatto and Windus, 1880, Volume I, page 204, as *Cooks, scullions – hear me, every mother's son*
Exhibited: Spink, London, as *Hanging on Every Word: Figures in an Inn*; 'De Verzameling Van Bernard Houthakker', Amsterdam Rijksmuseum, August-November 1964, no 87; 'Bliss was it in that dawn to be alive, 1750-1850', October 2008

All notes are written by Eleanor Hall, unless otherwise specified.

**Fierce as staring Ajax, from his seat**
**Uprose with visage stern, the king of meat**

Written by Rowlandson's friend and frequent supper companion, the satirist Dr John Wolcot (1738-1819) and published in 1786 under the nom-de-plume 'Peter Pindar', *The Lousiad* was 'an heroi-comic poem' in five Cantos, in which he ridicules the private life of King George III. The work took its name from a legend that a louse had once appeared on the King's dinner plate.

The Provenance for **02-03**, **07-08**, **13-24**, **26**, **29-43**, **48**, **50**, **56-58**, **60**, **63-64**, **66**, **71-73** and **75** is J Barton Townsend of Philadelphia

John Barton Townsend (1865-1928) was a prominent collector of illustrated books and caricatures from eighteenth and nineteenth-century Britain. His notable and extensive collection included drawings by Henry Alken, the three Cruikshanks (Isaac, George and Robert) as well as a great number of original works by Thomas Rowlandson. The collection was sold in a public auction at the American Art Galleries, New York, from 4 to 6 February 1919.

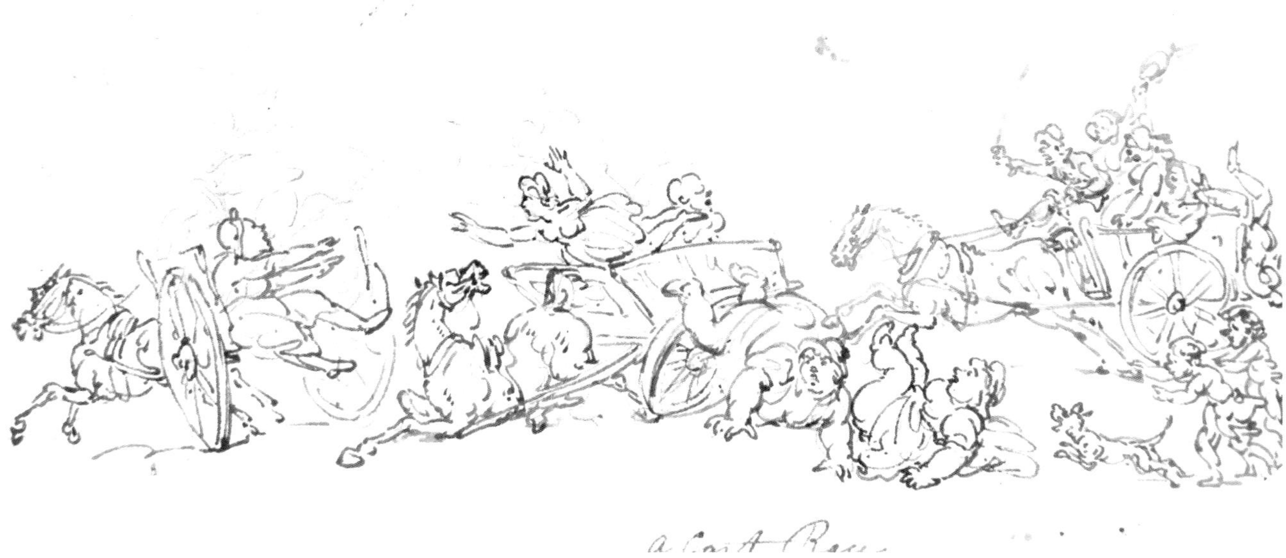

**02** A CART RACE
*inscribed with title*
*pen and ink with pencil*
*4 x 9 inches*

Preliminary drawing for *A Cart Race*,
published by William Holland, Oxford Street, 1789

Reverse:
A Cart Race
*traced drawing*
*3 ½ x 8 ¾ inches*

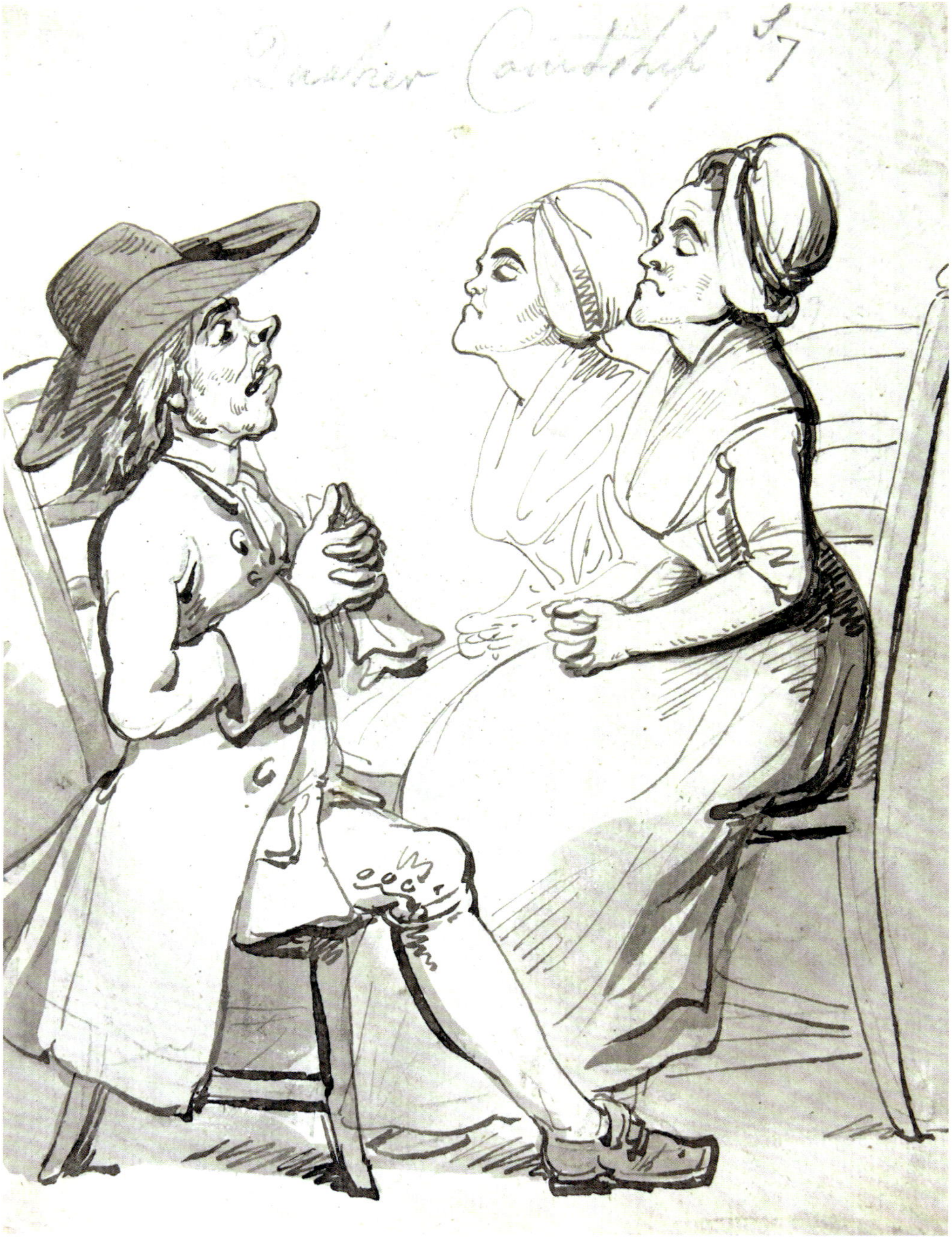




**03** QUAKER COURTSHIP
*inscribed with title*
*monochrome watercolour with pencil*
*9 ½ x 7 inches*

Reverse:
Group of Figures
*pencil*
*4 x 7 ½ inches*

**Quaker Courtship**

This may be the work that is listed in Grego as in his personal collection and titled *Quaker Courtship. Waiting for the Movement of the Spirit*. (See Joseph Grego, *Rowlandson the Caricaturist*, London: Chatto and Windus, 1880, Volume II, page 424)

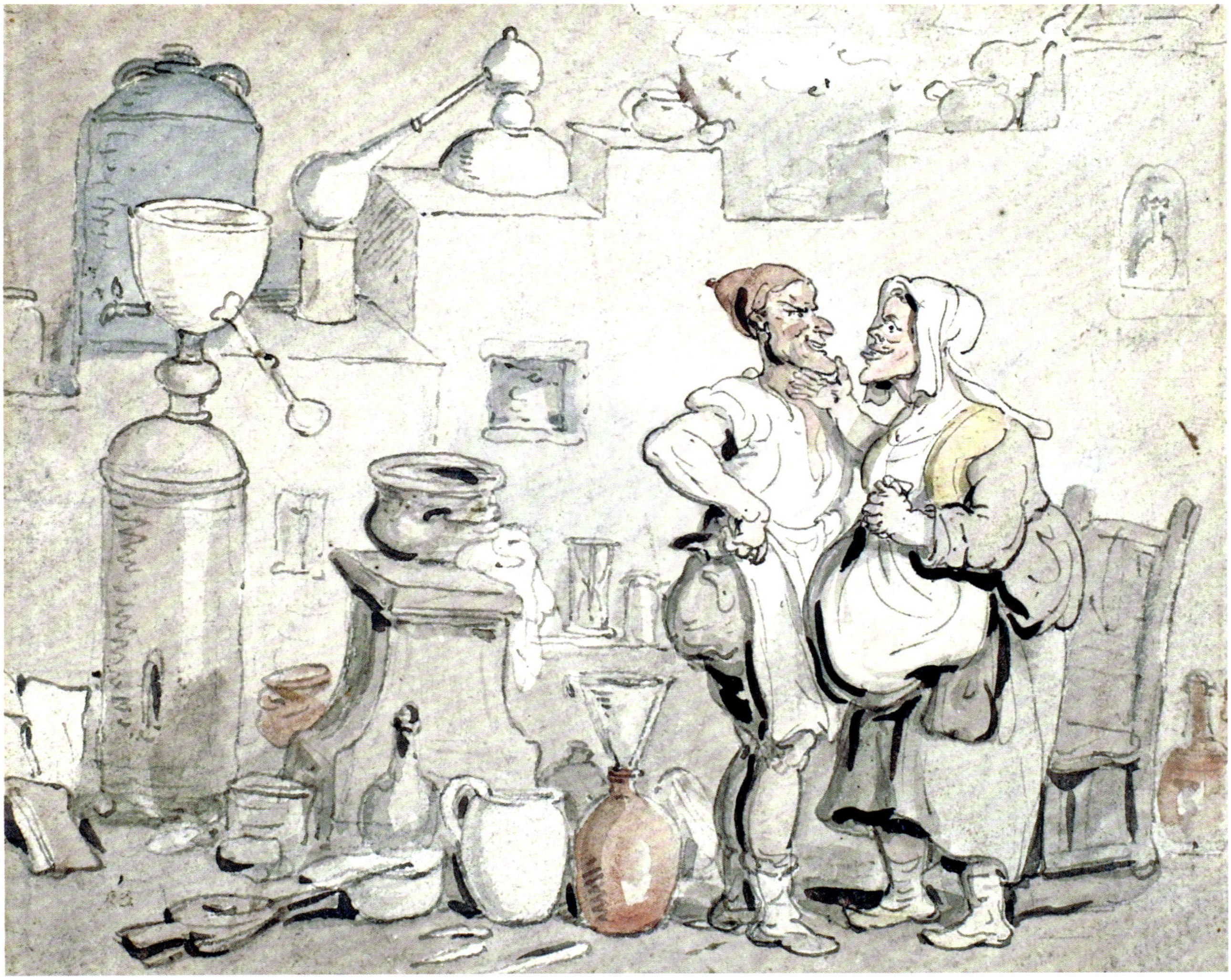



**04** THE ALCHEMY OF LOVE
*pen ink and watercolour*
*4 ¾ x 5 ¾ inches*

Exhibited: 'Bliss was it in that dawn to be alive, 1750-1850', October 2008, no 41

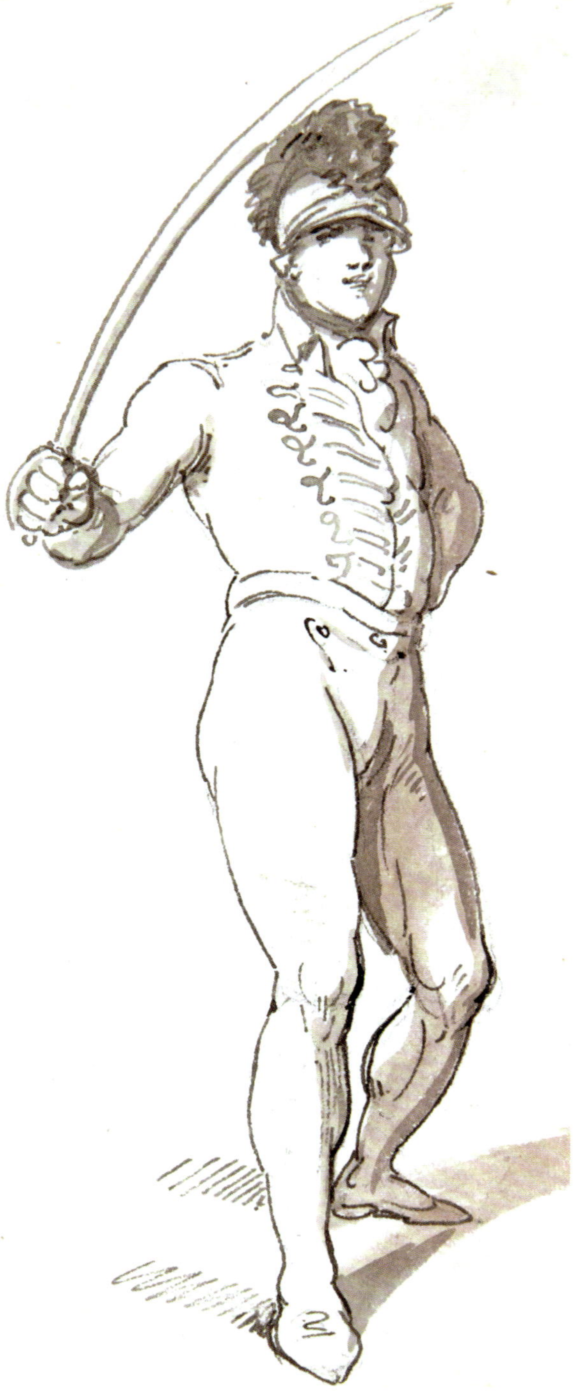

**05** OUTSIDE GUARD
*pen ink and watercolour with pencil*
*6 ½ x 3 inches*

Preliminary drawing for *Hungarian and Highland Broad Sword*, 24 plates designed and etched by Thomas Rowlandson, published by Henry Angelo, 1798

**Outside Guard**

Thomas Rowlandson produced a series of illustrations for *Hungarian and Highland Broad Sword*, an instruction manual in the art of sword combat. It was compiled by Rowlandson's close friend, Henry Angelo, and published in 1798. The son of the famous Italian fencing master, Domenico Angelo (1717-1802), Henry Angelo (1756-1835) was a renowned specialist in Hungarian broadsword and ran the fencing academy that appears in Rowlandson's *Madame Callee (Culloni) and M Renault in a Fencing Contest* [**68**]. Rowlandson depicted the implementation of a Hungarian broadsword, more commonly known as a sabre, in battle, with officers in various different combat positions and stances.

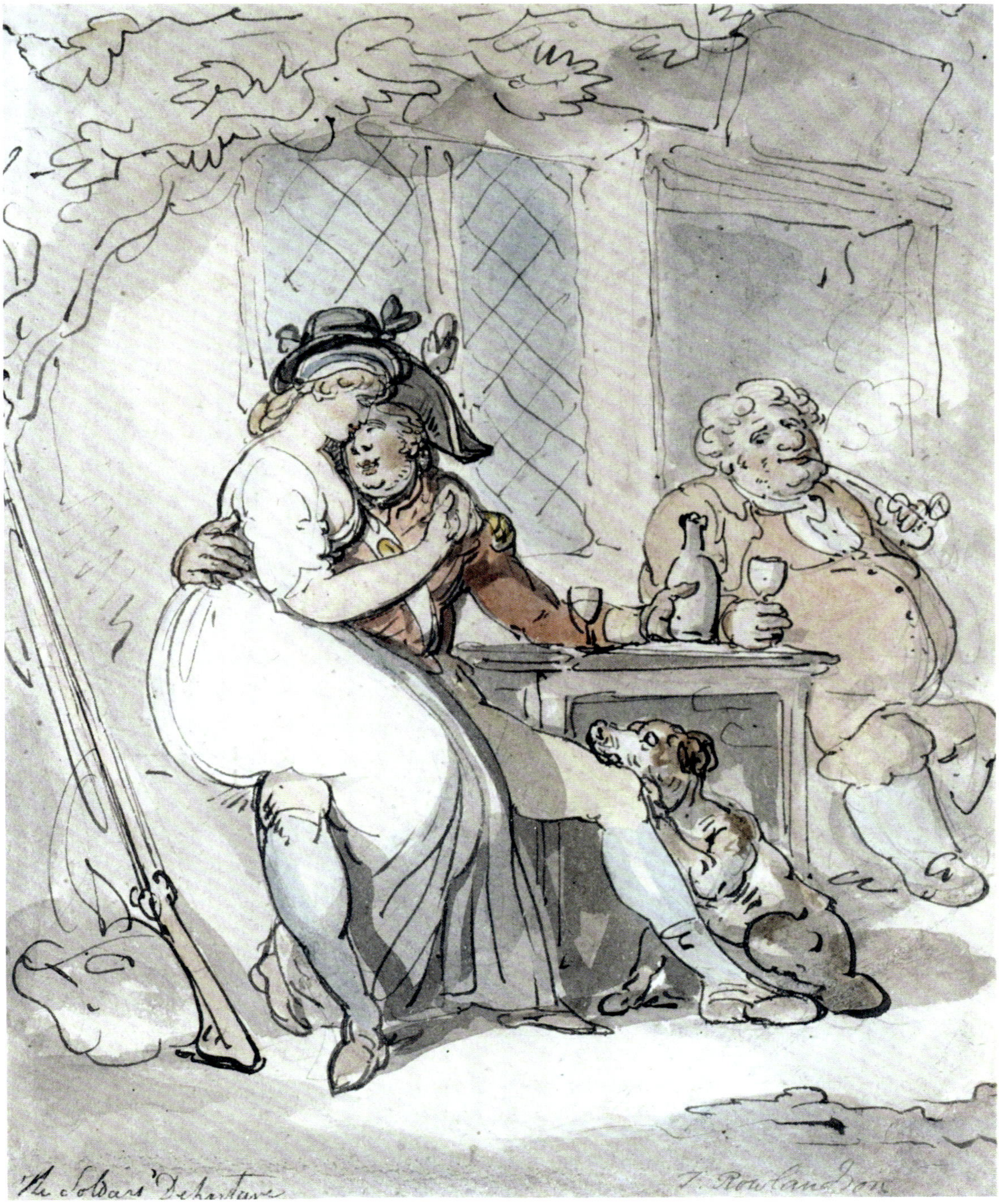




**06** THE SOLDIER'S DEPARTURE
*signed and inscribed with title*
*pen ink and watercolour*
*8 ¼ x 6 ¾ inches*

Published by Rudolph Ackermann, 1 September 1796
Exhibited: 'Bliss was it in that dawn to be alive, 1750-1850',
October 2008, no 45

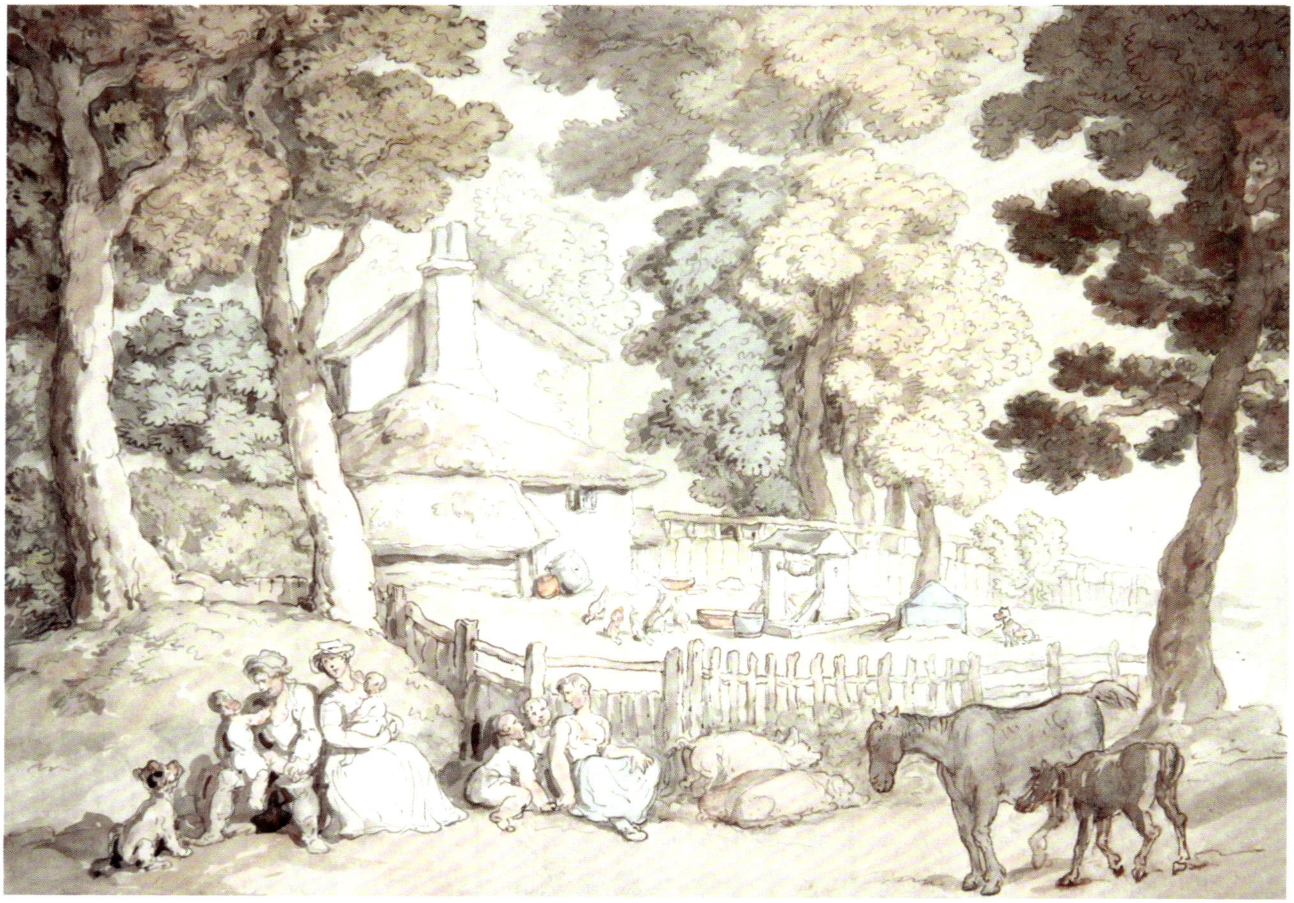

**07** RUSTIC IDLENESS
*pen ink and watercolour*
*8 ½ x 12 inches*

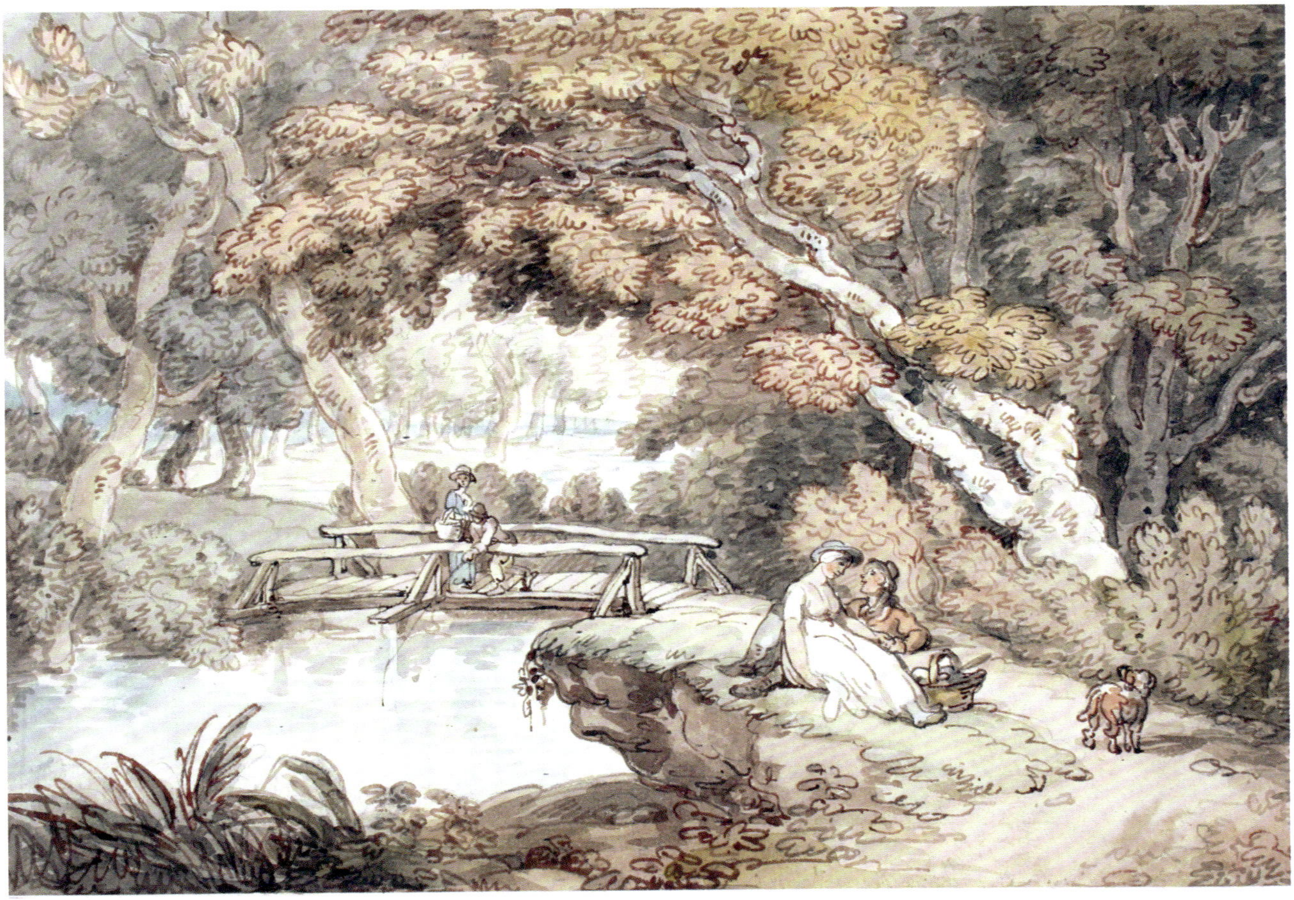

**08** A SYLVAN IDYLL
*pen ink and watercolour*
*7 x 10 ¼ inches*

Exhibited: 'Bliss was it in that dawn to be alive, 1750-1850', October 2008, no 56

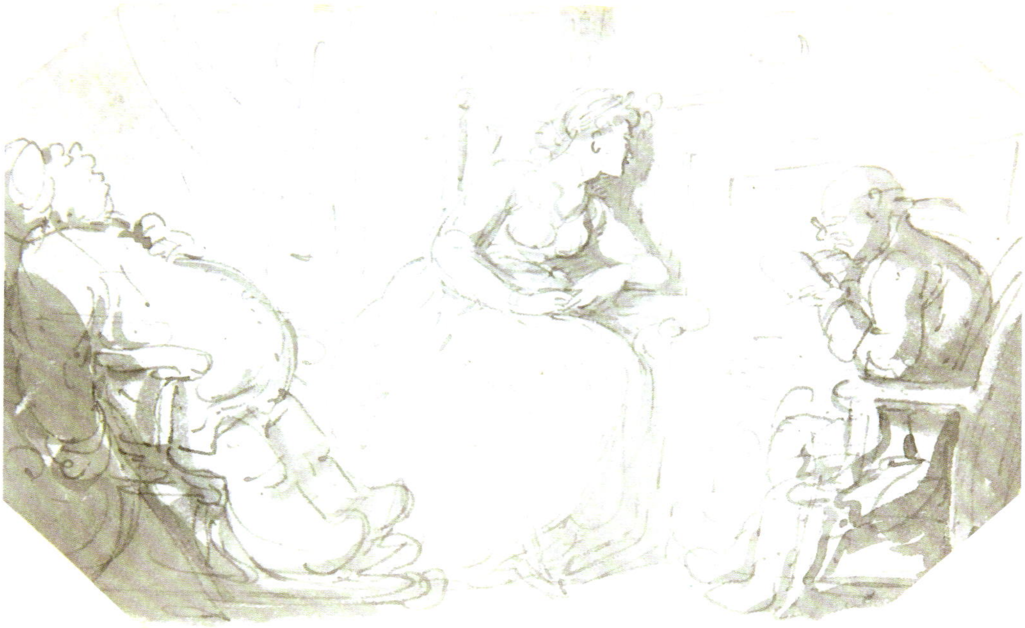

**09** EVENING REST
*pen ink and monochrome watercolour*
*4 ½ x 7 inches*

Reverse:
Buying a Gravestone
*pencil*
*6 ½ x 4 inches*

**Evening Rest**

This may be a preparatory sketch for *The Comforts of Bath*, a series of satirical drawings by Rowlandson, published in 1798. These drawings were based on the picaresque novel, *The Expedition of Humphry Clinker*, written by Tobias Smollett and published in 1771. The novel was presented in the form of letters written by six different characters, including a Welsh Squire named Matthew Bramble. Rowlandson's drawings depict Matthew Bramble on a visit to the spa town of Bath in an attempt to cure his health, and follow his various activities in order to satirise gently the fashionable society that he finds there.



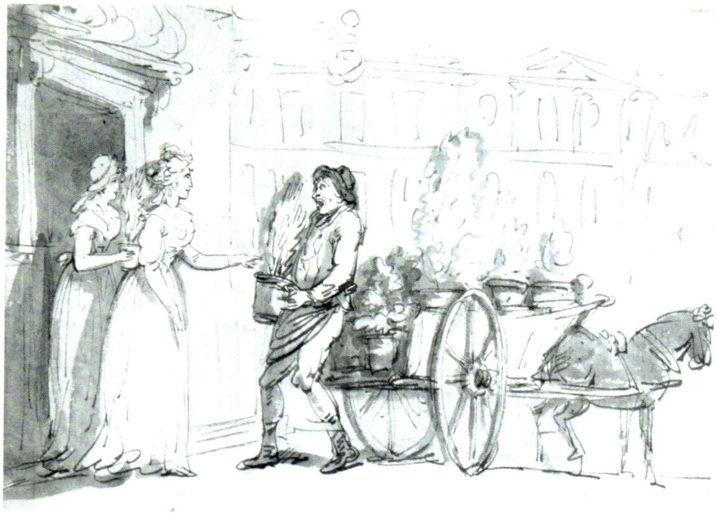

**10** THE PLANT SELLER
*pen ink and monochrome watercolour*
*4 ½ x 6 ¼ inches*

Preliminary drawing for *Cries of London, no 6. All a-growing, a-growing; Here's flowers for your gardens*, published by Rudolph Ackermann, 1799

**The Plant Seller**

The image of the urban plant seller, offering his wares from door to door, forms part of a series known as the *Cries of London*, which Rowlandson illustrated for publication by Ackermann in 1799.
The idea of depicting London's 'lower orders', as street vendors and door-to-door tradesmen, and the characteristic shouts and cries that accompany the bustle of the streets, has been popular with writers and artists for over 300 years. Francis Wheatley's *Cries of London* was a series of paintings exhibited at the Royal Academy between 1792-95. The paintings were full of idealistic and somewhat sentimental images of the urban poor and were made popular by a contemporary series of prints. In contrast, Rowlandson's *Cries* satirised this sentimentality with a much more honest and critical view of these vendors.

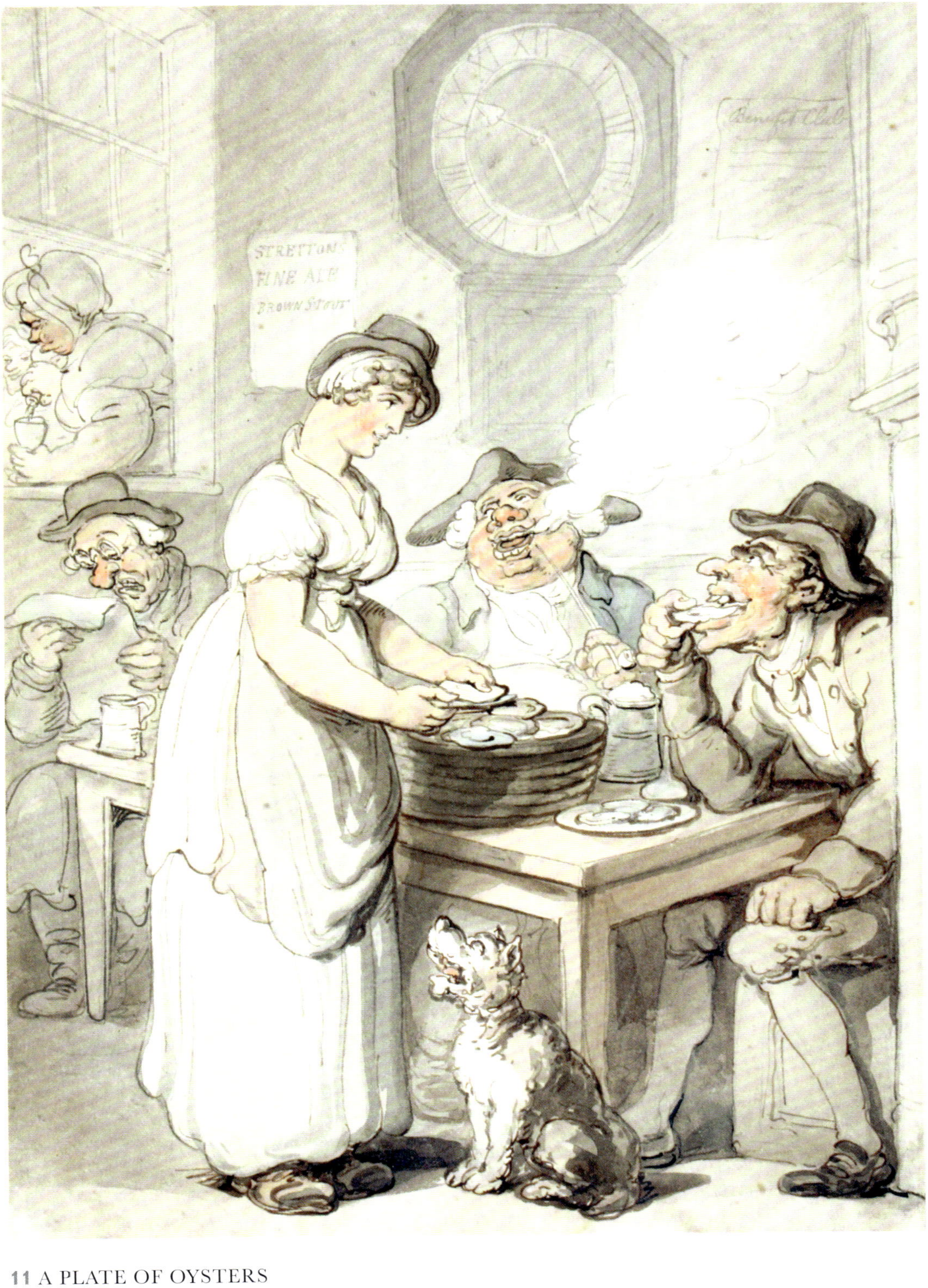




**11** A PLATE OF OYSTERS

*pen ink and watercolour*

*12 ¾ x 9 ¼ inches*

Exhibited: 'Bliss was it in that dawn to be alive, 1750-1850', October 2008, no 43

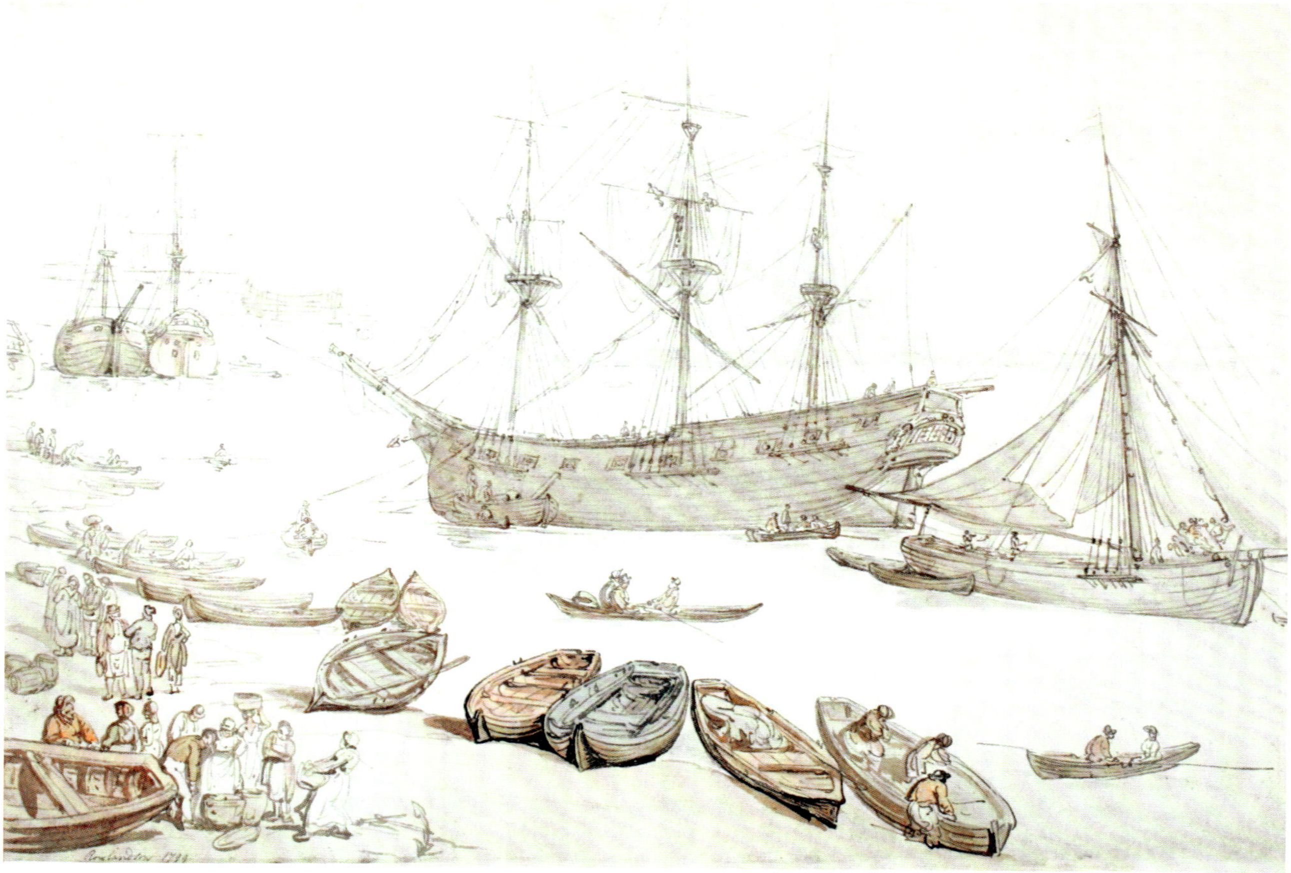



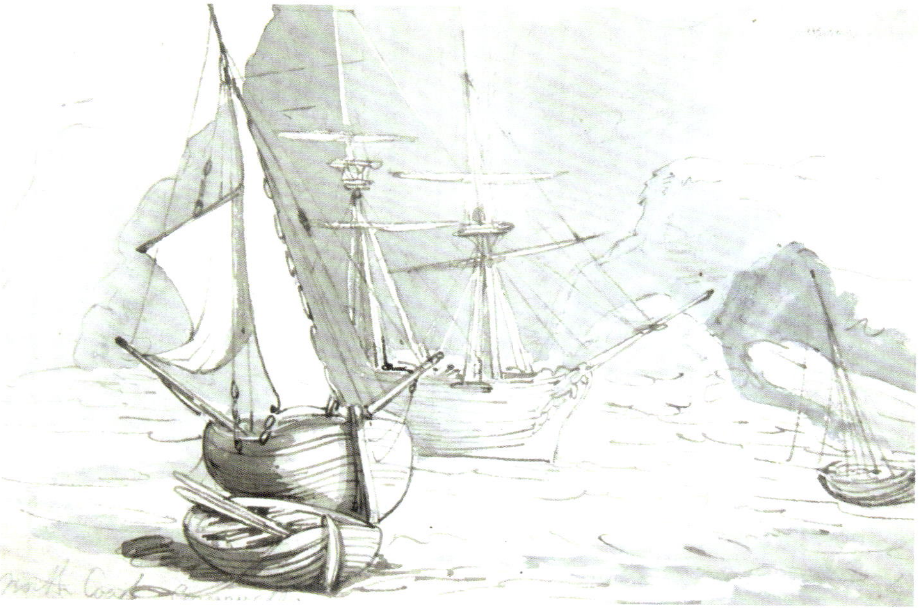

**12** UNLOADING THE SHIPPING
*signed and dated 1799*
*pen ink and watercolour*
*12 x 17 inches*

Exhibited: 'Bliss was it in that dawn to be alive, 1750-1850', October 2008, no 54

**13** NORTH COAST, CORNWALL
*inscribed with title*
*pen ink and watercolour with pencil*
*6 x 8 ¼ inches*

Reverse:
Mocking the Man
*pencil*
*5 ½ x 8 inches*

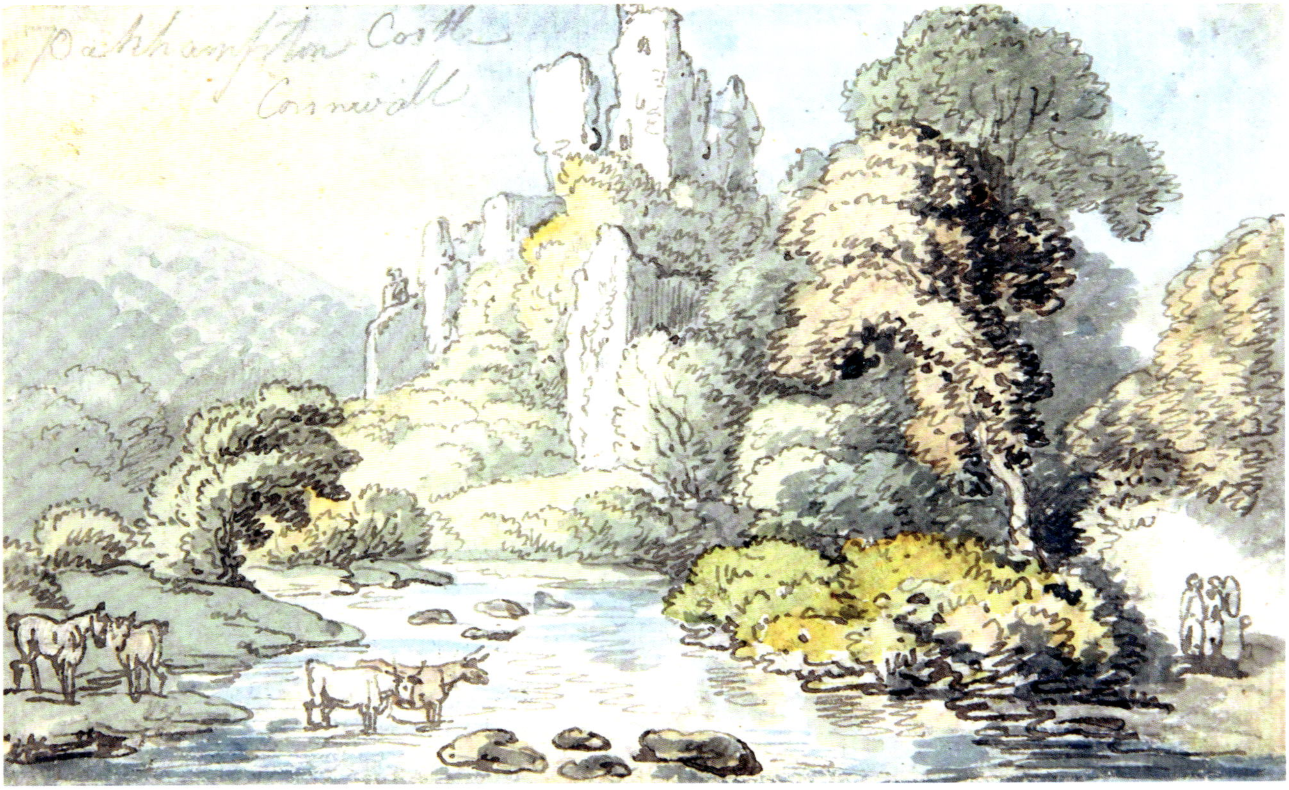



**14** OAKHAMPTON CASTLE, CORNWALL
*inscribed with title*
*pen ink and watercolour with pencil*
*4 x 6 ¼ inches*

Rowlandson visited the West Country a number of times, staying with his friend and major patron, Matthew Michell, who was a banker and Deputy Lieutenant of Cornwall. En route, he stopped at the Devon town of Okehampton, and drew its picturesque ruin of a motte and bailey castle (though he misspelt its name, and mistook its location).

There is a similar, more elaborate watercolour titled *Okehampton Castle*, illustrated in V P Sabin *A Catalogue of Watercolour Drawings by Thomas Rowlandson (1756-1827)*, London, 1933, page 41. The description given in the catalogue relates equally to the present work:

> To the right are the tree embowered remains of the ancient castle of Okehampton, with the ruins of the keep on the summit of a conical hill; in the centre is the valley of the Okement River, which can be seen in the foreground tumbling over boulders, whilst to the left the hills are clothed in dense foliage; in the centre background a distant view of Dartmoor.

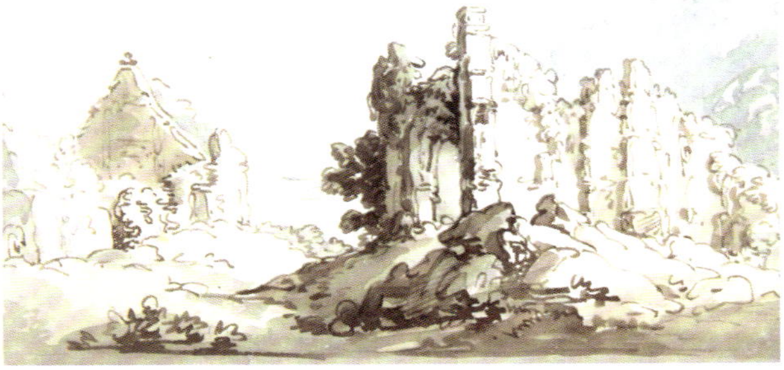

**15** OAKHAMPTON PRIORY, CORNWALL
*inscribed with title*
*pen ink and monochrome watercolour with pencil*
*7 ¼ x 8 ¼ inches*

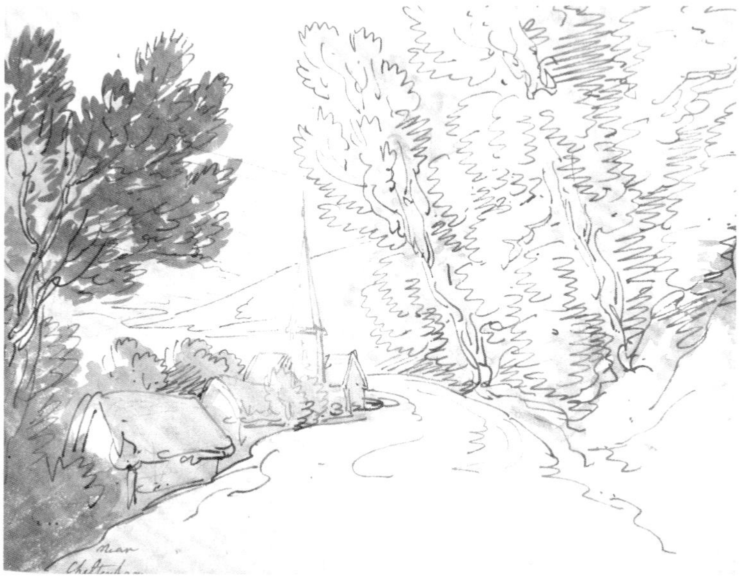

**Near Cheltenham**

Rowlandson's inscriptions on the reverse of this image suggest that he may also have visited Oxford around this time. It is quite possible that he passed through Oxford on his way to Cheltenham, and made a note of the places he wished to see there. His handwritten note lists the Museum Arundelianum and the Schola Logicae and Moralis Philosophiae, both of which form part of the University of Oxford. The Schola Logicae and Moralis Philosophiae was once located in the building that now houses part of the Bodleian Library. The Museum Arundelianum was a room, adjoining the Old Schools Quadrangle, used to house the Arundel Collection of Greek marbles, collected in the early seventeenth century by Thomas Howard, 21st Earl of Arundel. Some of the marbles have important inscriptions upon them, such as the Parian Chronicle, which is a Greek chronological table covering the years from 1581 BC to 264 BC. The collection is now in the Ashmolean Museum.

**16** NEAR CHELTENHAM
*inscribed with title*
*inscribed 'Museum Arundelianum' and 'Sch Logicae & Mor Philosophiae' on reverse*
*pen ink and monochrome watercolour with pencil*
*6 x 7 ¾ inches*



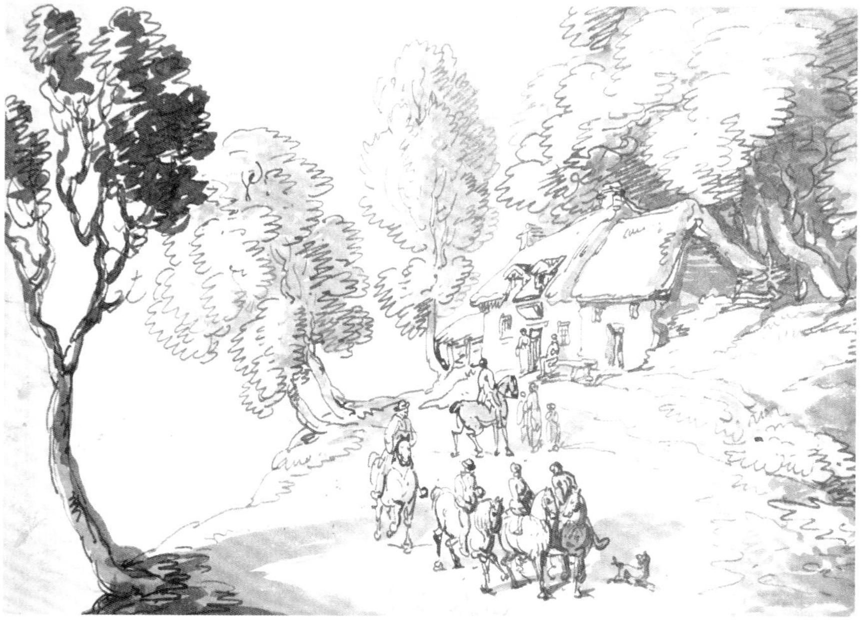

**South Wales**

Rowlandson visited Wales on a picturesque tour in August 1797, accompanied by his friend Henry Wigstead. Although the pair intended it as a pleasure trip, Rowlandson made a series of descriptive sketches, and it is probable that this view of South Wales is from this time. These sketches were later combined with Wigstead's own journal notes, to form the book *Remarks on a Tour to North and South Wales in the year 1797*, which was published in 1800. (See Joseph Grego, *Rowlandson the Caricaturist*, London: Chatto & Windus, 1880, Volume I, page 360)

**17** SOUTH WALES
*inscribed with title*
*watercolour testing on reverse*
*pen ink and monochrome watercolour with pencil*
*5 ¾ x 8 inches*

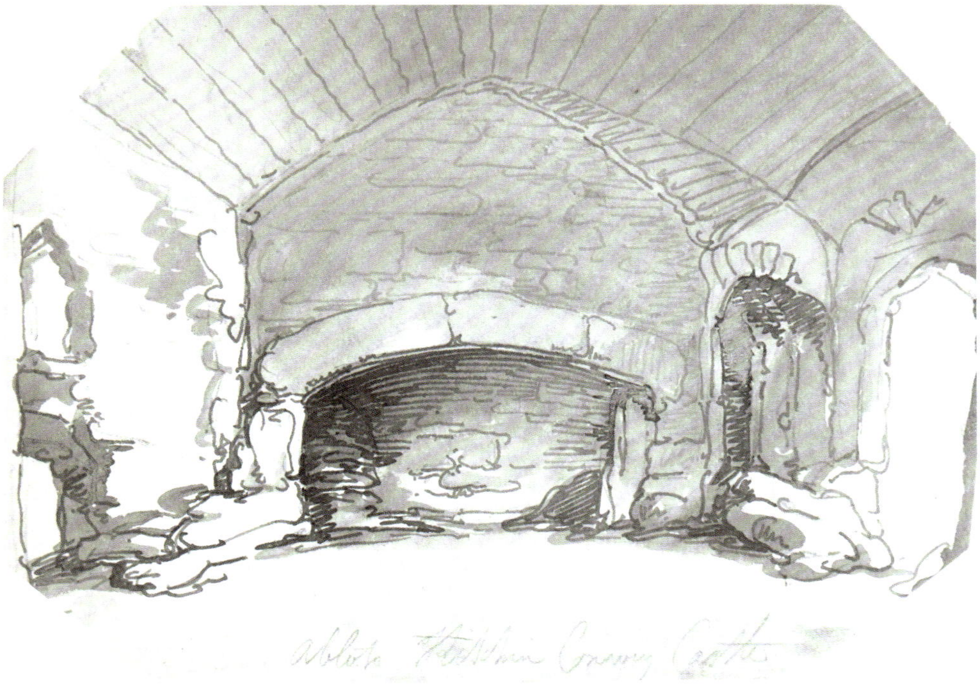

**18** ABBOTS KITCHEN, CONWAY CASTLE
*inscribed with title*
*pen ink and monochrome*
*watercolour with pencil*
*6 x 8 ½ inches*



**Entrance to Conway Castle**

Rowlandson made a number of studies of this thirteenth-century fortress, one of which is strikingly similar to the present work and dated circa 1797. This is now in the collection of The National Library of Wales.

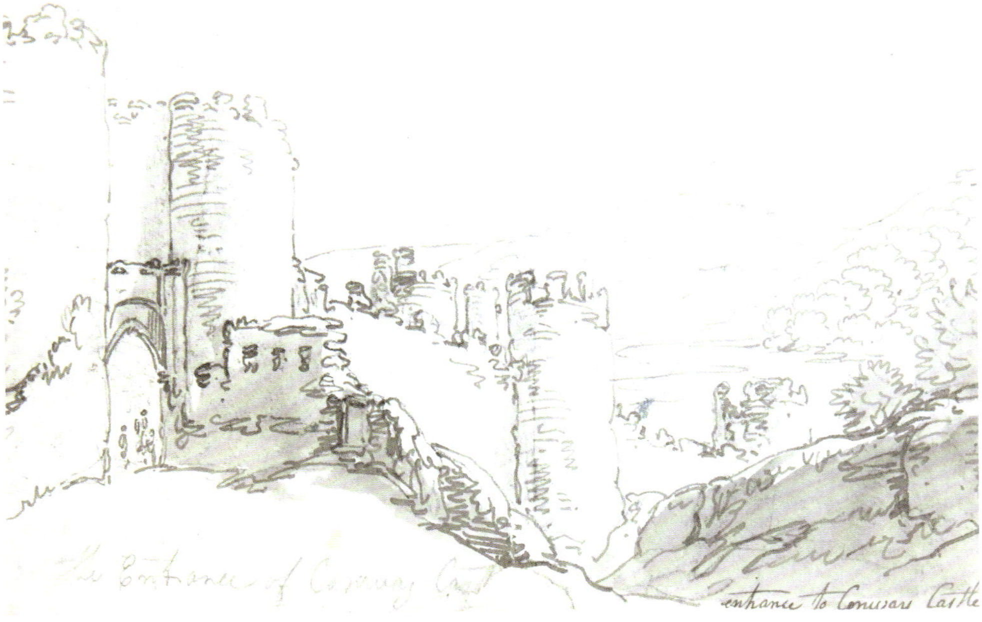

**19** ENTRANCE TO CONWAY CASTLE
*inscribed with title and 'The entrance of Conway Castle'*
*pen ink and monochrome*
*watercolour with pencil*
*4 ¾ x 7 ¼ inches*

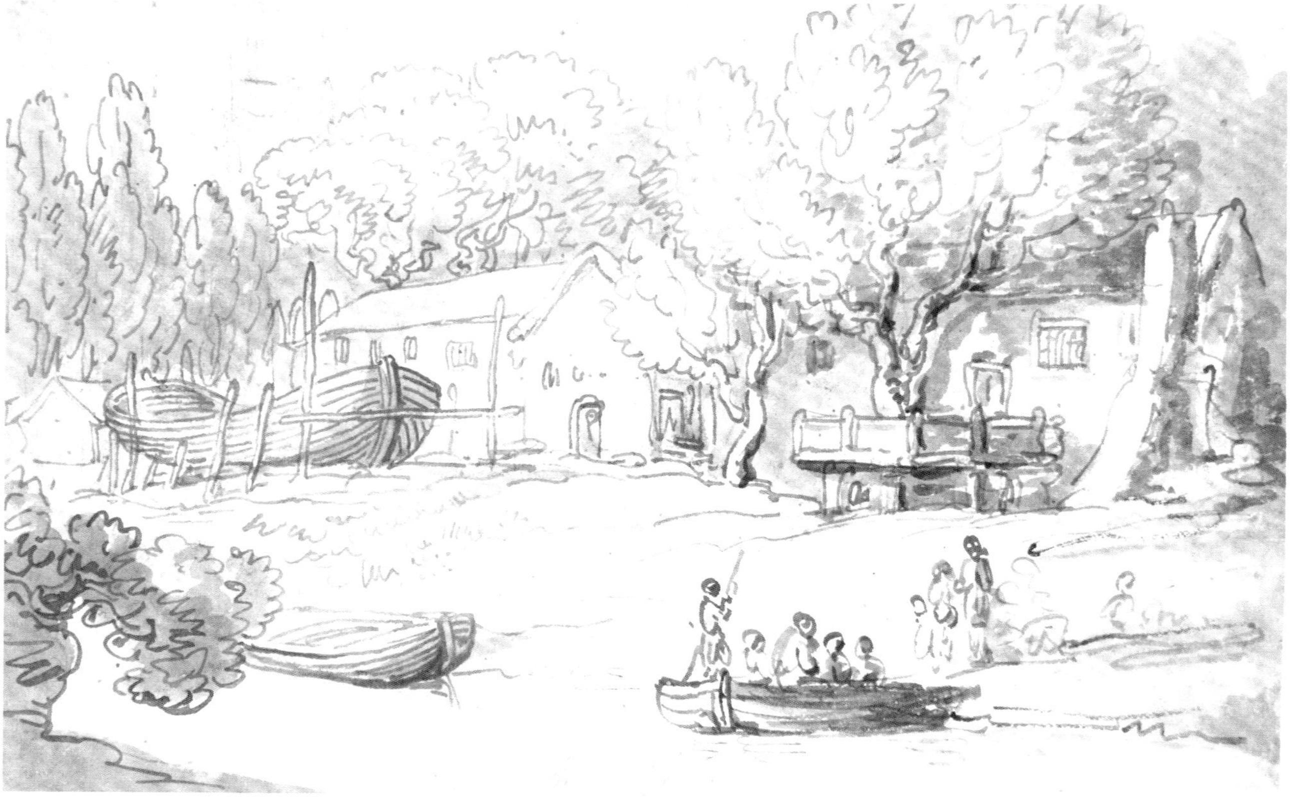

**20** DONCASTER
*inscribed with title and 'Y-'*
*pen ink and monochrome watercolour with pencil*
*4 ½ x 7 ½ inches*

Reverse:
Crowds and Carriages
*pencil*
*4 ½ x 7 ¼ inches*

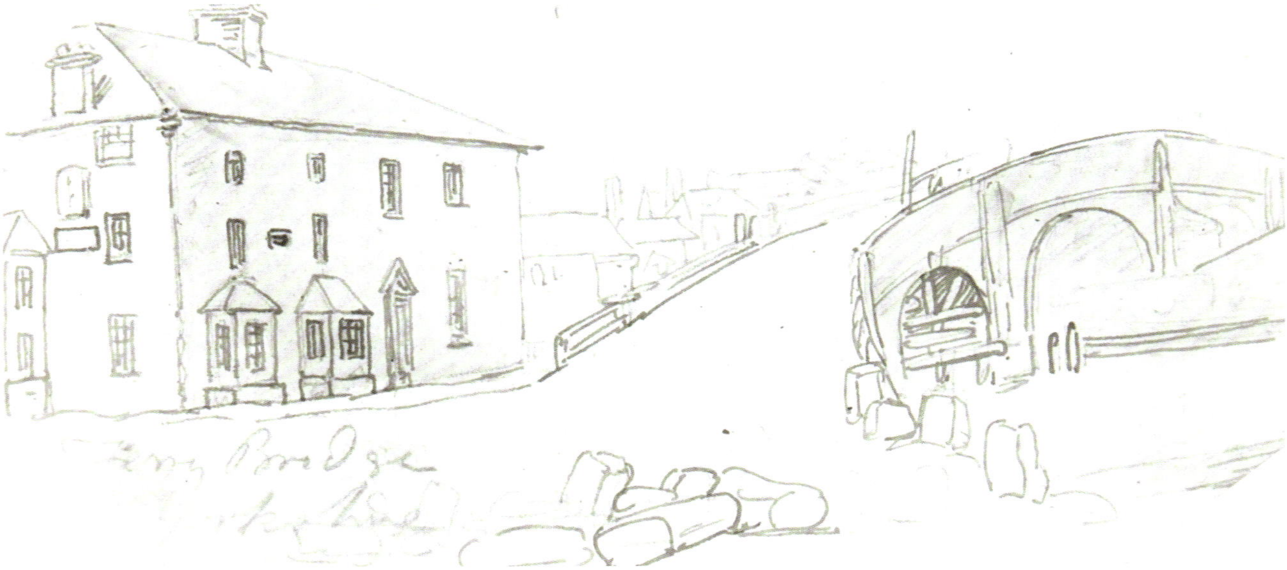

**21** FERRY BRIDGE, YORKSHIRE
*inscribed with title*
*pen ink and monochrome watercolour with pencil*
*3 ¼ x 7 inches*

Reverse:
Two Naked Figures
*pencil*
*3 x 7 inches*



**22** MICKLEGATE, YORK
*inscribed with title*
*pen ink and watercolour with pencil*
*4 ¼ x 9 ¼ inches*

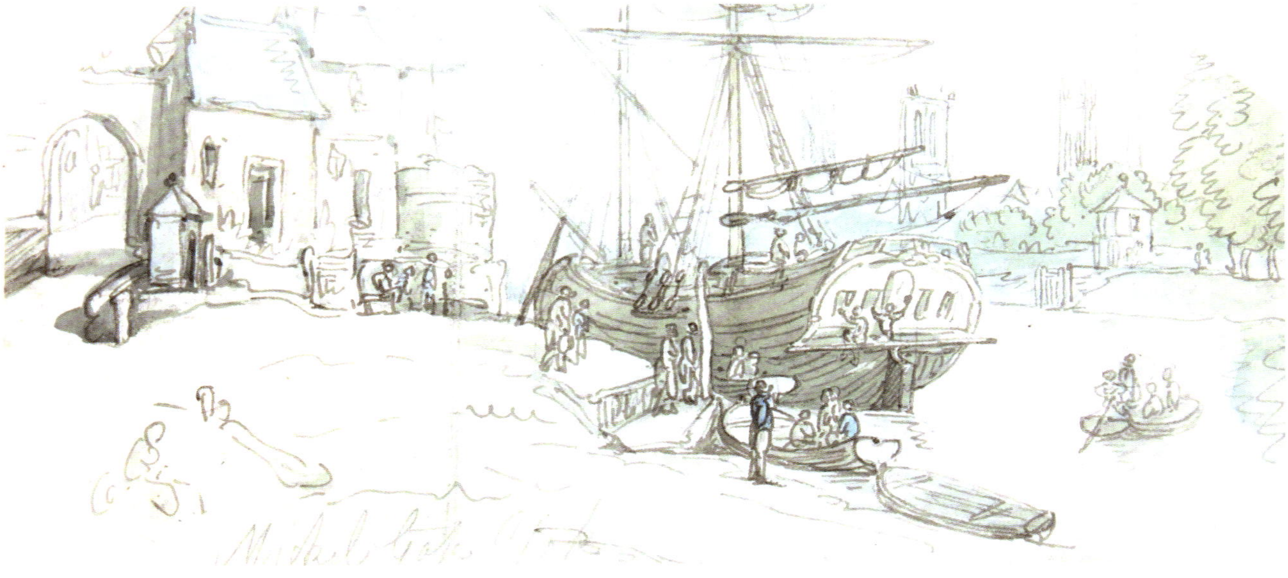

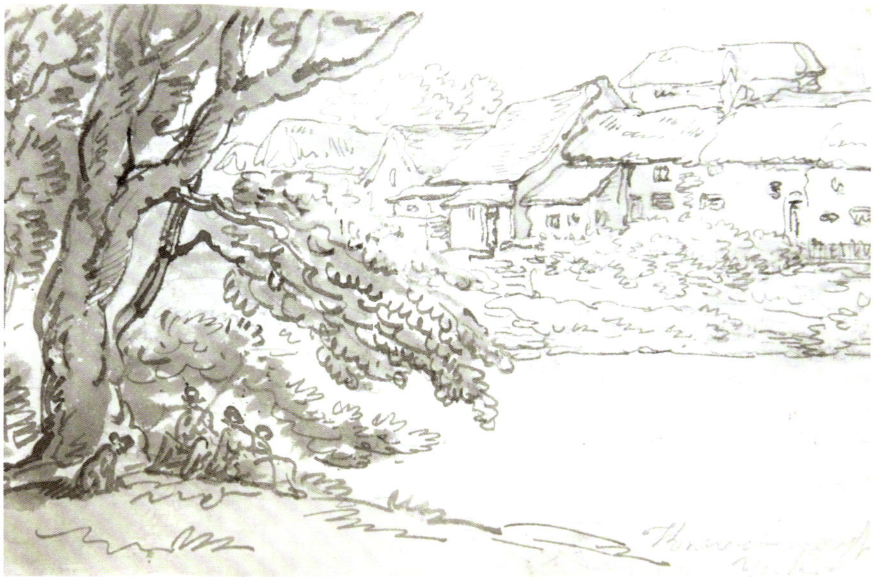

**23** KNARESBOROUGH, YORK
*inscribed with title*
*pen ink and monochrome watercolour with pencil*
*4 ½ x 6 ½ inches*



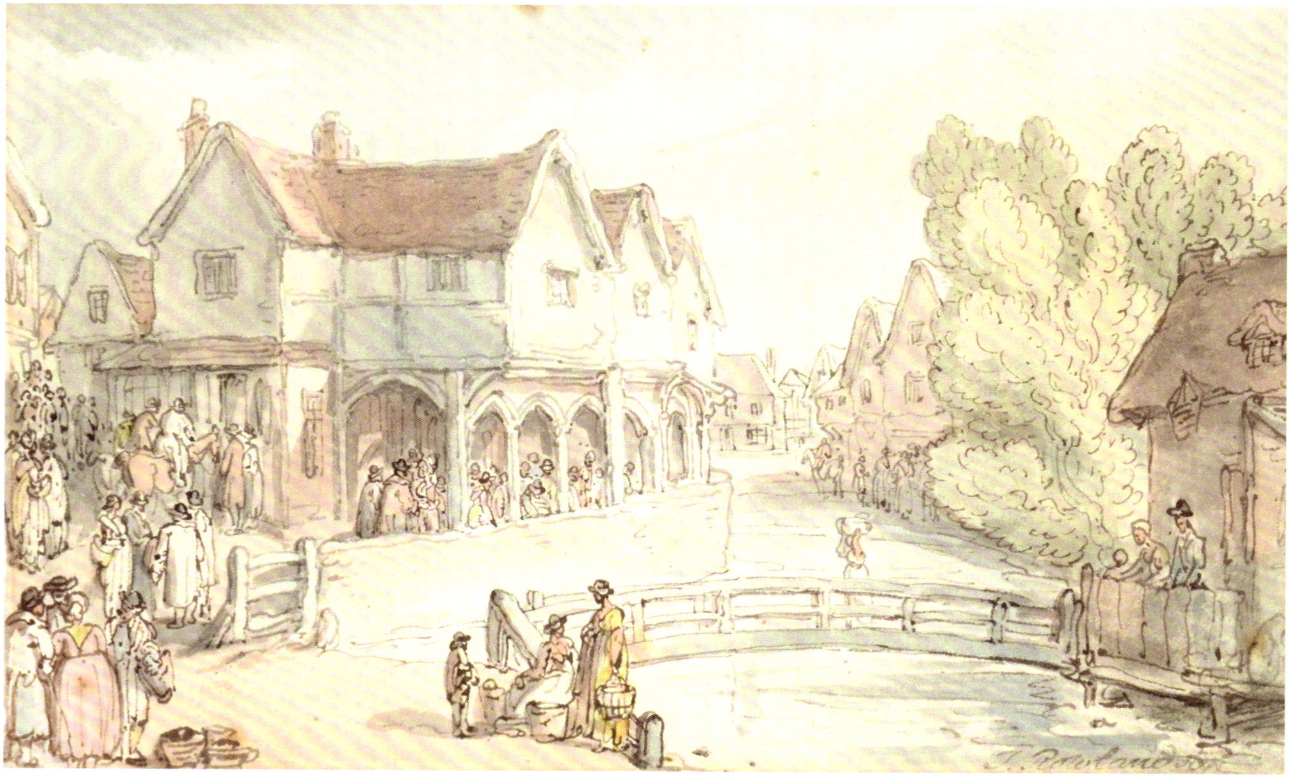

**24** STREET SCENE
*inscribed 'T Rowlandson' in another hand*
*pen ink and watercolour*
*5 ¾ x 9 ¼ inches*

Similar to *Country Town*, exhibited in 'Thomas Rowlandson (1756-1827)', Frank T Sabin, 154 New Bond Street, 1933, no 99

Reverse:
Seated Man
*pencil, 9 x 5 ½ inches*

**25** SIGHTSEEING
*pencil*
*4 ¾ x 7 ¼ inches*

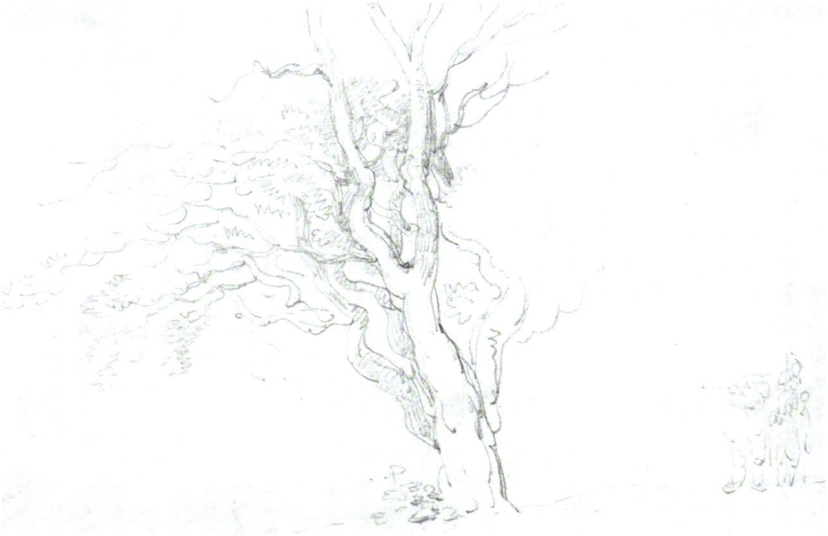



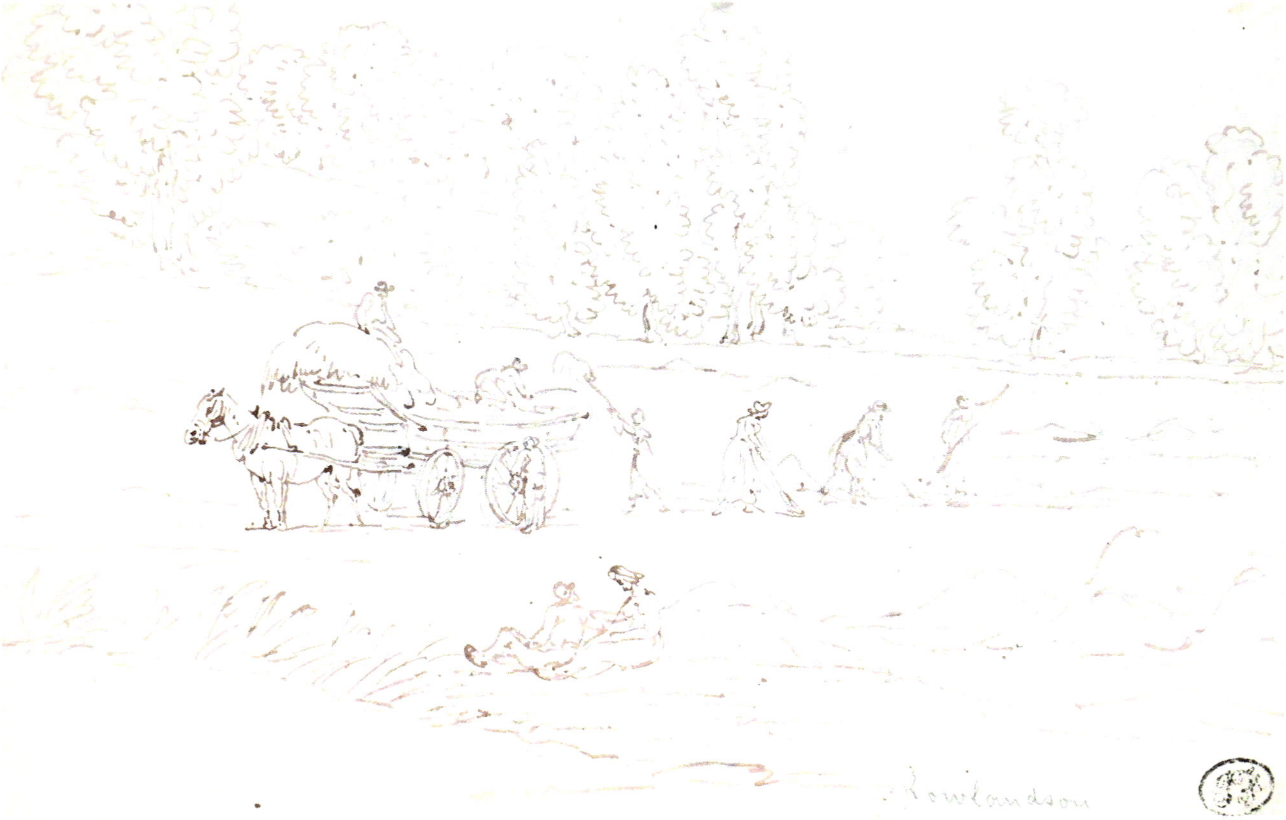


**26** HAYMAKING
*inscribed 'Rowlandson' and stamped with the collector's mark of John Fitchett Marsh*
*pen and ink with pencil*
*4 ¾ x 7 ¼ inches*

Provenance: John Fitchett Marsh

The Lancashire solicitor, John Fitchett Marsh (1818-1880), is best remembered as an antiquary and promoter of municipal libraries. His own collection – including 'Drawings by the Old Masters, Engravings, Paintings, Silver Plate, and Articles of Virtu' as well as an 'Extensive Library' was sold at Sotheby's in 1882. **DW**

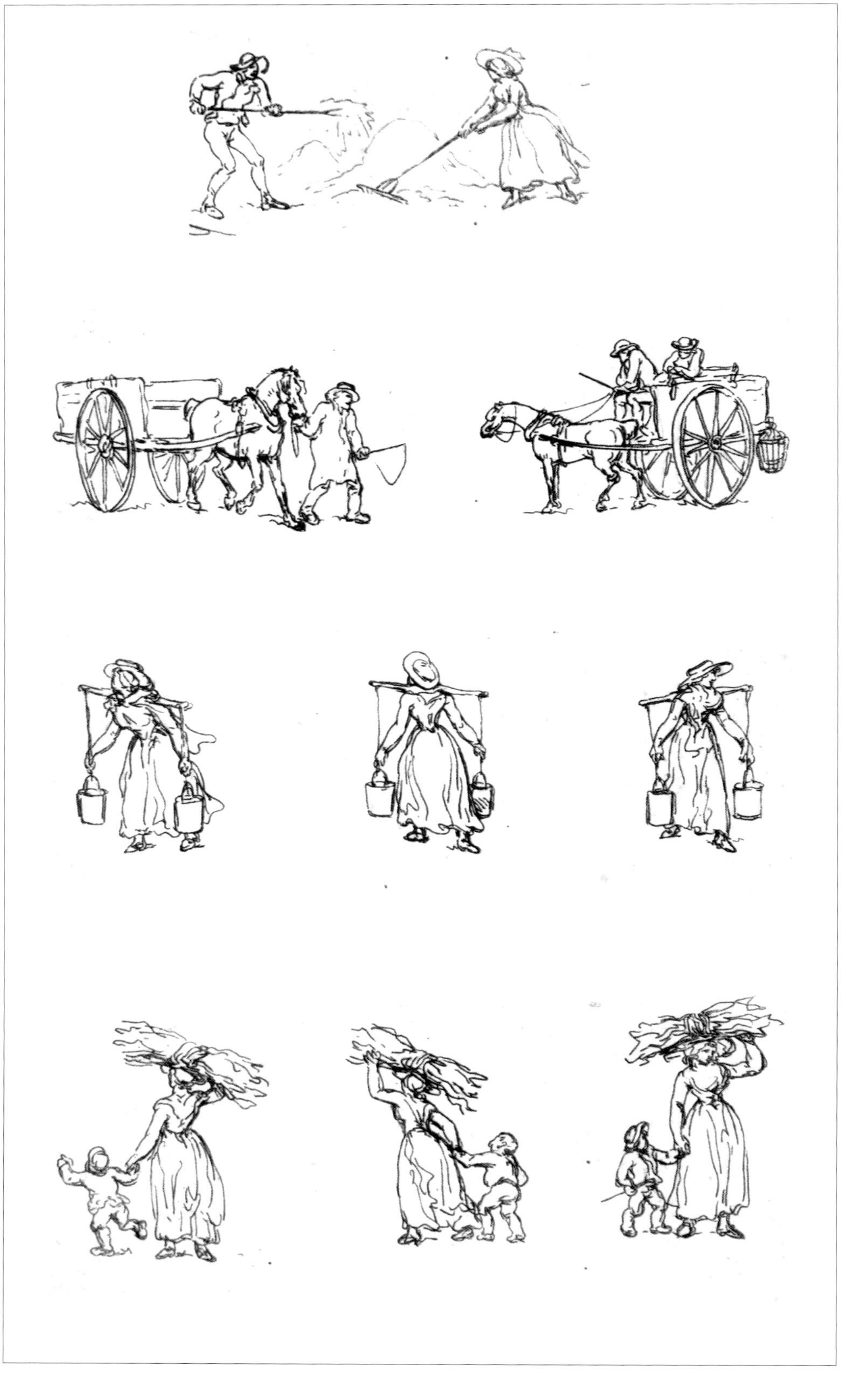

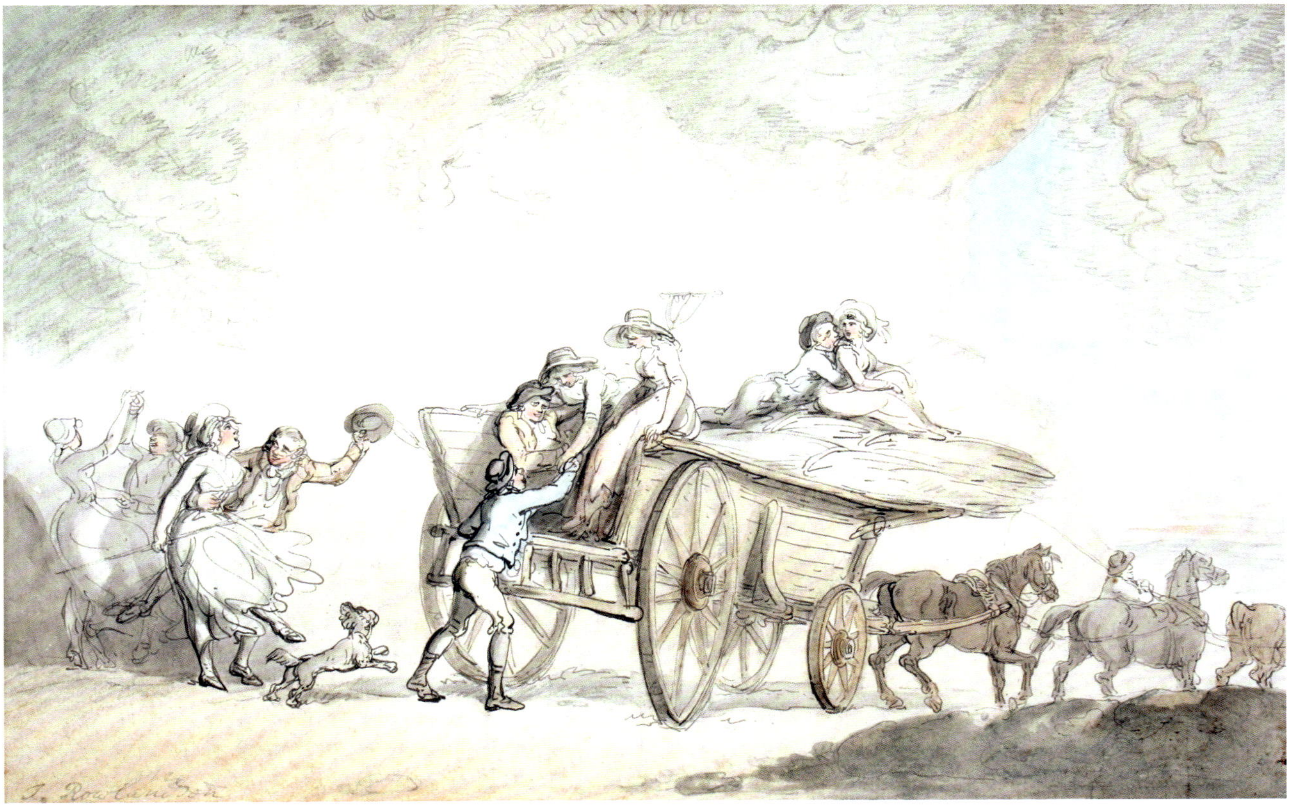

**28** HARVESTERS MERRYMAKING
*signed*
*watercolour*
*9 ¾ x 15 inches*

Exhibited: 'Bliss was it in that dawn to be alive, 1750-1850', October 2008, no 36

**27** MINIATURE STUDIES (opposite)
*inscribed 'Rowlandson SC' in another hand*
*series of etchings*
*8 x 5 inches*

Literature: Joseph Grego, *Rowlandson The Caricaturist*, London: Chatto and Windus, 1880, Volume I, pages 7, 30, 40, 41, 43, 54 and 87

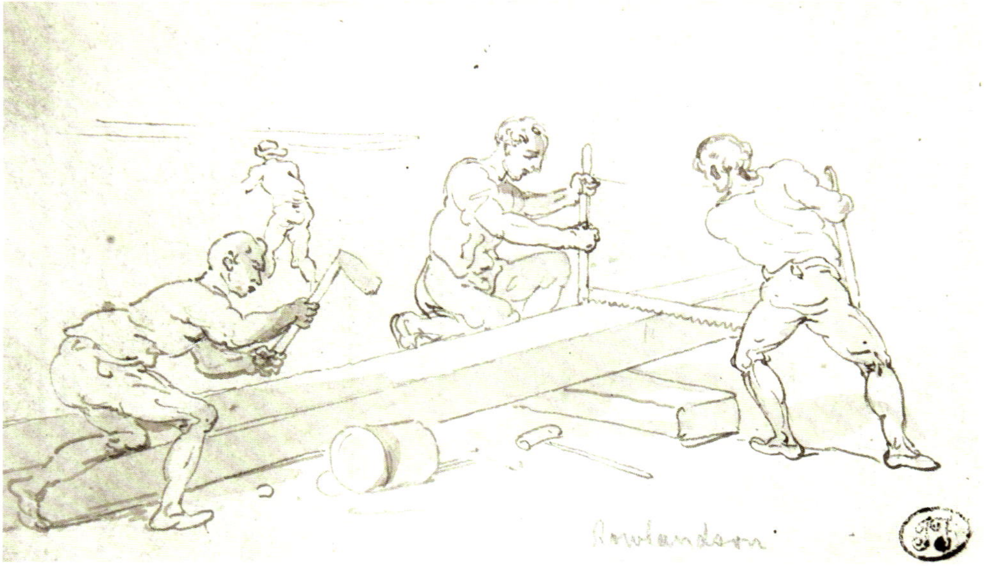


**29** THE HAND THAT CANNOT BUILD A HOVEL MAY DEMOLISH A TEMPLE
*inscribed 'Rowlandson' in another hand and stamped with the collector's mark of John Fitchett Marsh*
*inscribed with title on reverse*
*pen ink and watercolour with pencil, 3 ¼ x 5 ½ inches*

Provenance:
John Fitchett Marsh

The title is believed to have originated in a saying by Samuel Johnson.



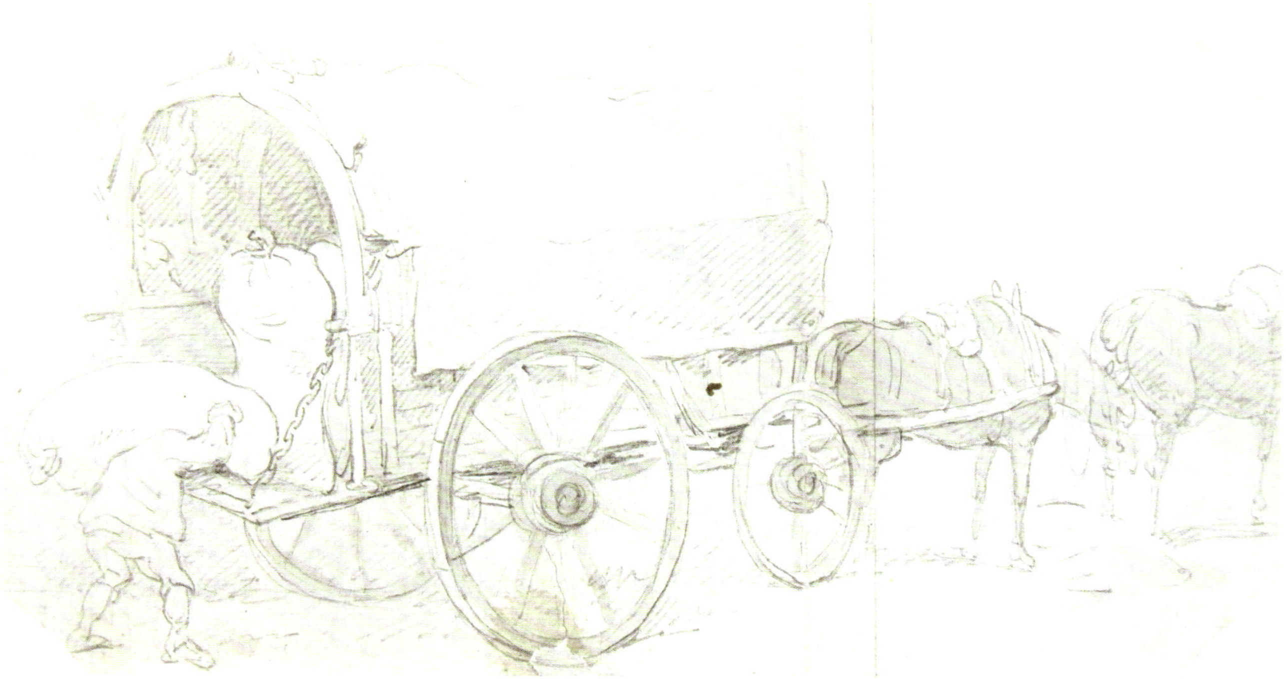

**30** LOADING THE CART
*pencil with monochrome watercolour*
*5 ½ x 10 inches*

**Mr Canning**

Rowlandson's portrayals of society scandals and his caricatures of notorious aristocrats and leading politicians ridiculed the intricacies of Georgian London. George Canning, who served as Foreign Secretary for the Tory Party (1807-1809 and 1822-1827) and then briefly as Prime Minister in 1827, would have been well known by his contemporaries since his rapid rise in politics during the mid 1790s. His charisma and remarkable skills as an orator meant that he soon became a prominent figure, dividing opinion amongst those in his party and gathering a group of supporters known as 'Canningites' around him.

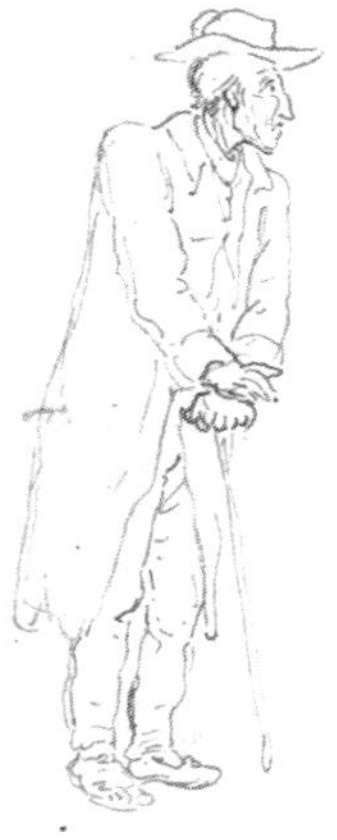

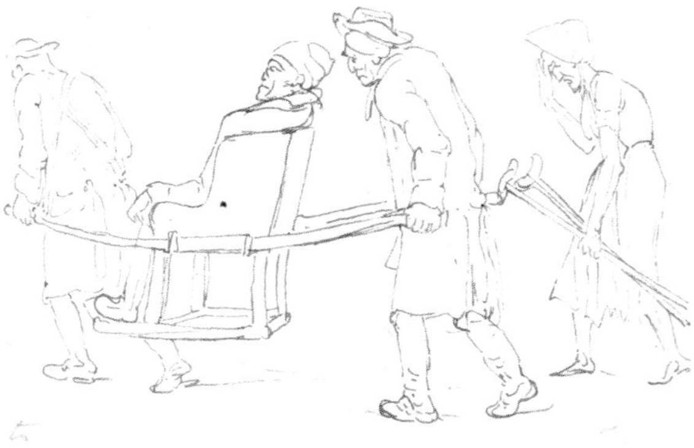

**31** FROM A GARRET TO A WORKHOUSE
*inscribed with title*
*pen and ink with pencil*
*5 x 7 ½ inches*

Reverse:
Mr Canning
*inscribed with title*
*pencil*
*7 ½ x 5 inches*



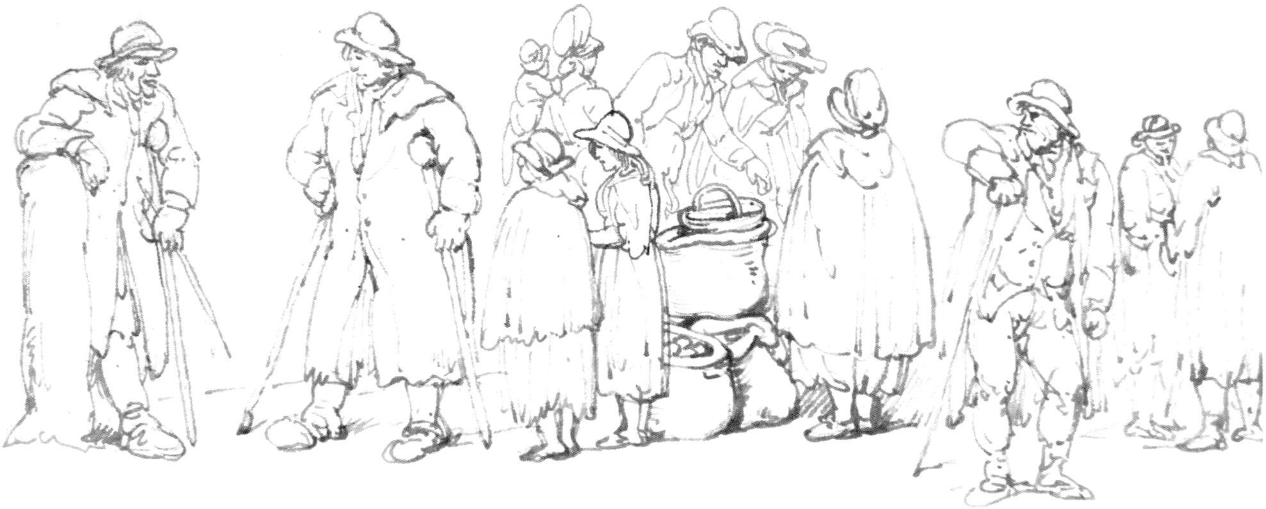

**32** SICK AND LAME
*pen and ink with pencil*
*3 ½ x 7 ¾ inches*

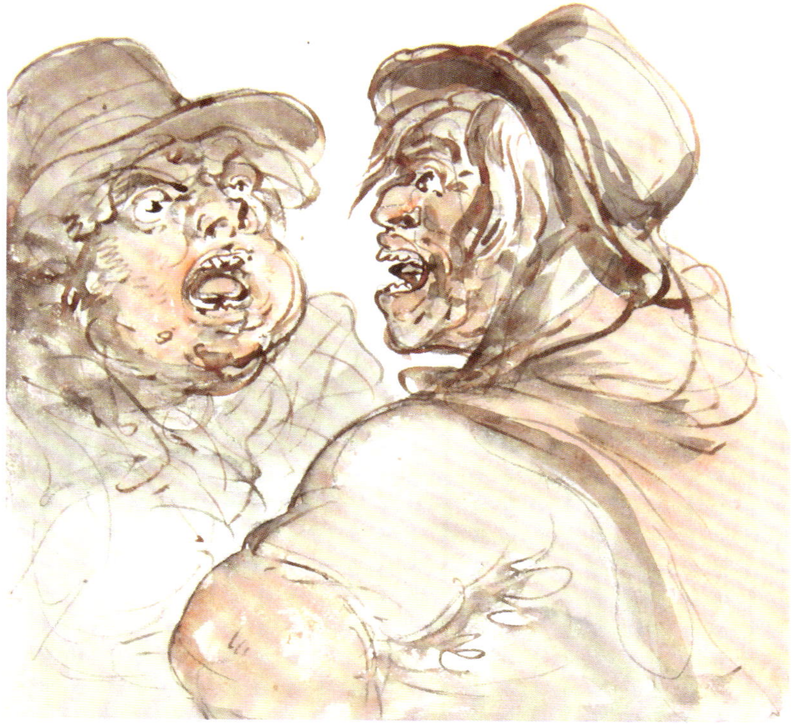

**33** A BRACE OF FISH HAGS
*inscribed with title*
*pen ink and watercolour with pencil*
*7 ¼ x 6 ¾ inches*

**34** BOXING
*pen ink and watercolour with pencil*
*4 ½ x 8 inches*

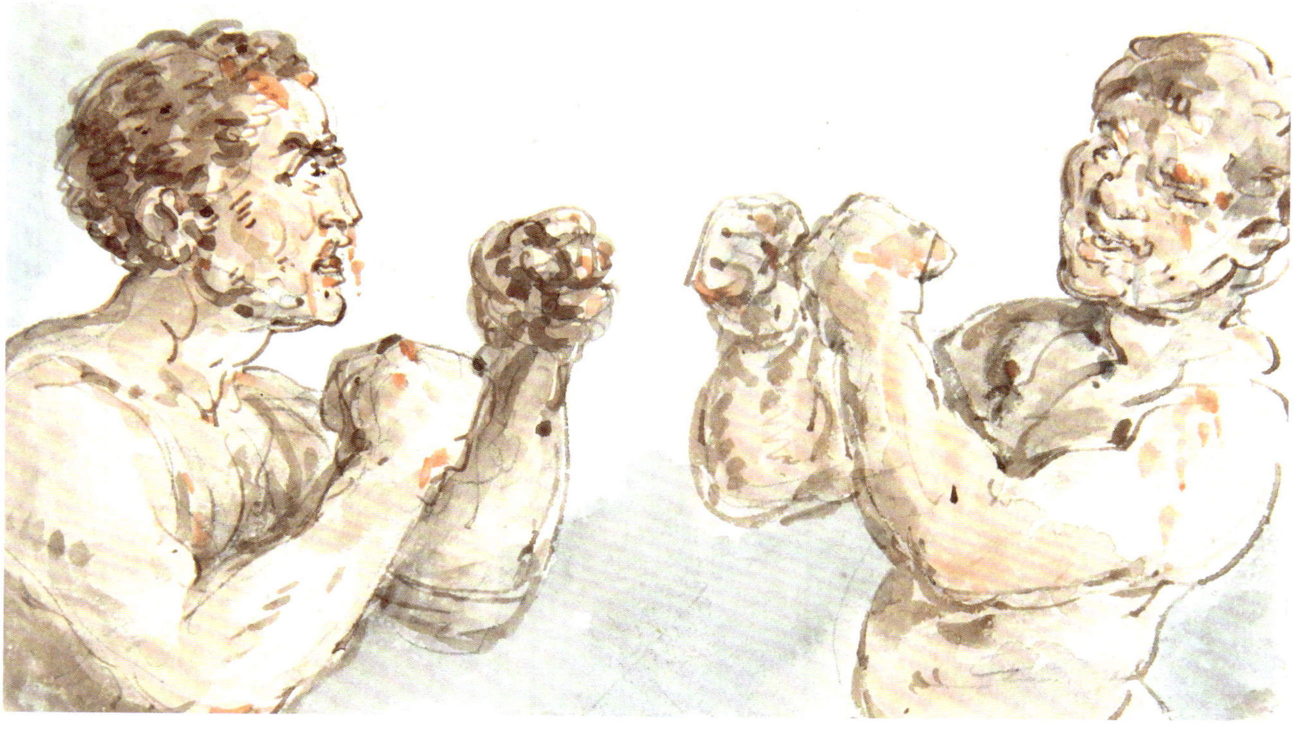

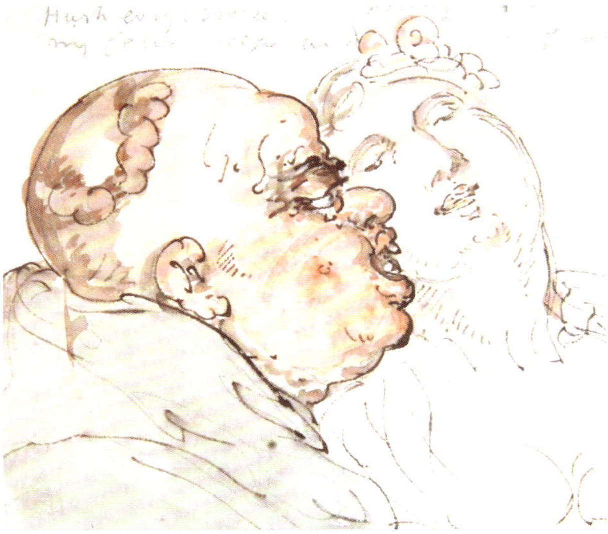

**35** HUSH EV'RY BREEZE, LET NOTHING MOVE, MY CELIA SLEEPS AND DREAMS OF LOVE
*inscribed with title*
*pen ink and watercolour with pencil*
*4 ¾ x 5 ¼ inches*

The title is taken from a popular song by James Hook first published about 1780.

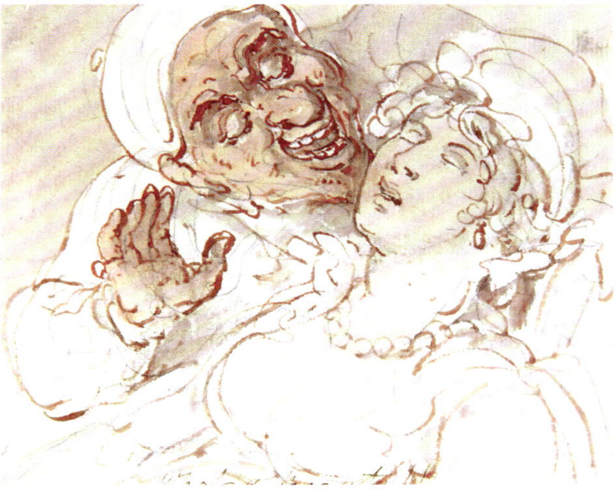

**36** WHAT A BEAUTY
*inscribed with title*
*pen ink and watercolour with pencil*
*4 ¾ x 6 inches*



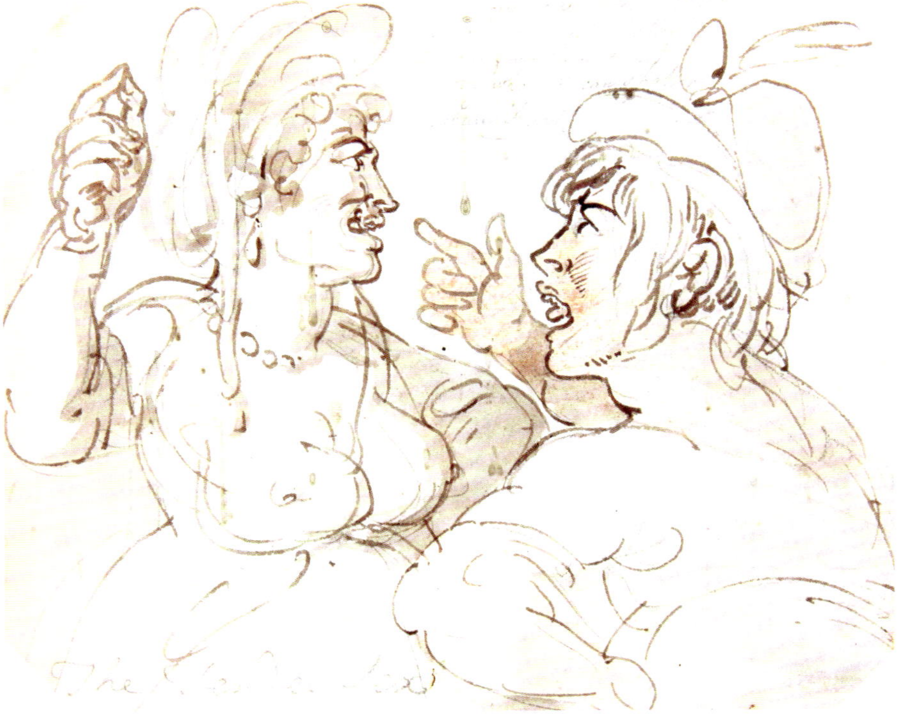

**37** THE TENDER SEX
WHY HOW NOW, MADAM FLIRT
IF YOU THUS MUST CHATTER
AND ARE FOR FLINGING DIRT
LETS TRY WHO BEST CAN SPATTER
MADAM FLIRT
*inscribed with title*
*pen ink and watercolour with pencil*
*5 ¾ x 7 inches*

The title includes lines taken from John Gay's *The Beggar's Opera*, 1728.

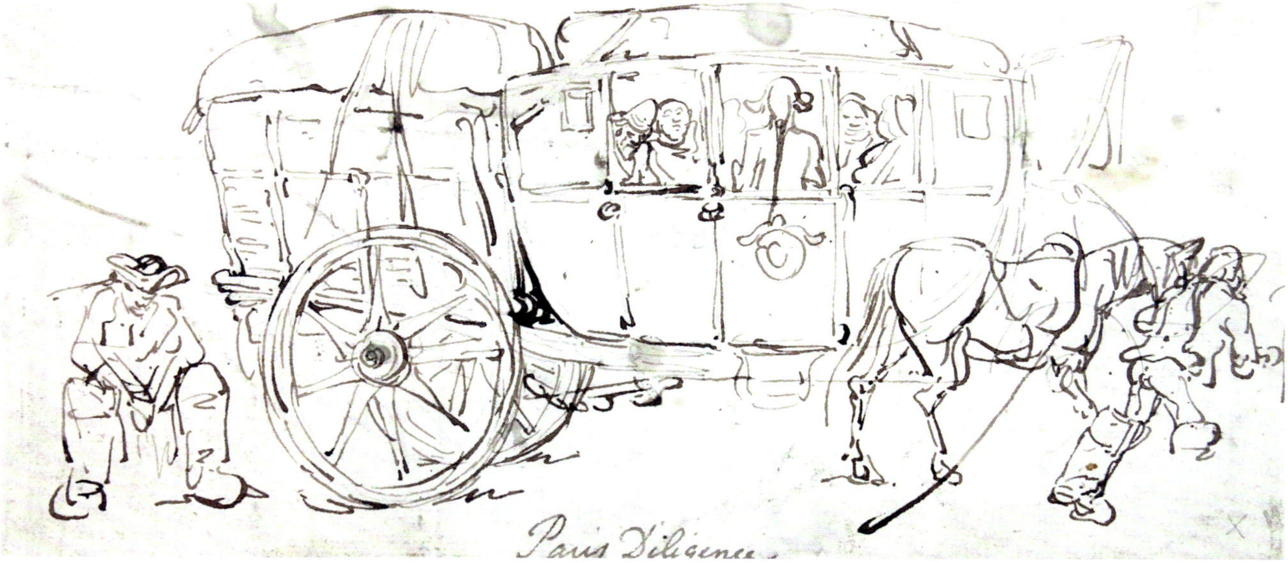


**38** PARIS DILIGENCE
*inscribed with title*
*watercolour testing on reverse*
*pen and ink with pencil*
*4 ¾ x 10 ½ inches*



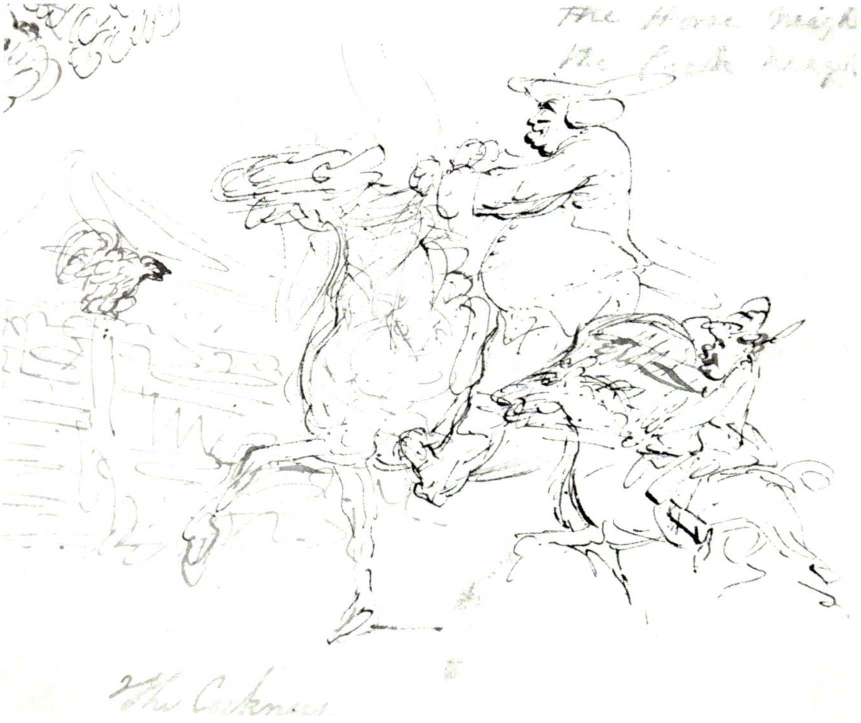

**39** THE COCKNEY
*inscribed with title and 'The Horse Neighs The Cock Neighs'*
*inscribed 'The Horse Neighs The Cock Neighs' on reverse*
*pen and ink*
*5 x 6 inches*

Reverse:
Legs and Wheels
*pencil*
*5 x 6 inches*

**40** THE FIDDLER AND HIS FAMILY
*pen ink and watercolour with pencil*
*8 ½ x 5 ¾ inches*

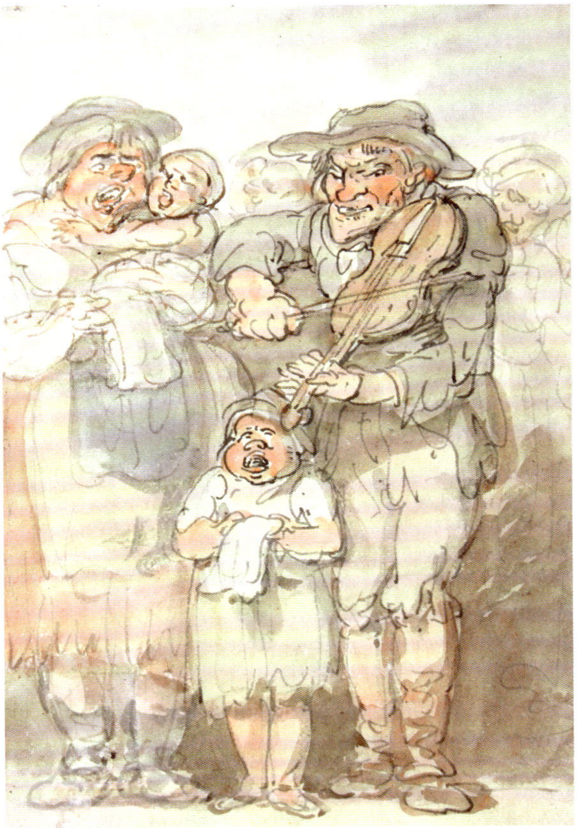

**41** O MY
*inscribed with title*
*pen ink and monochrome watercolour with pencil*
*5 ¾ x 9 ¼ inches*

Reverse:
O My
*traced drawing and watercolour testing*
*pencil with pen ink and watercolour*
*5 ½ x 9 inches*



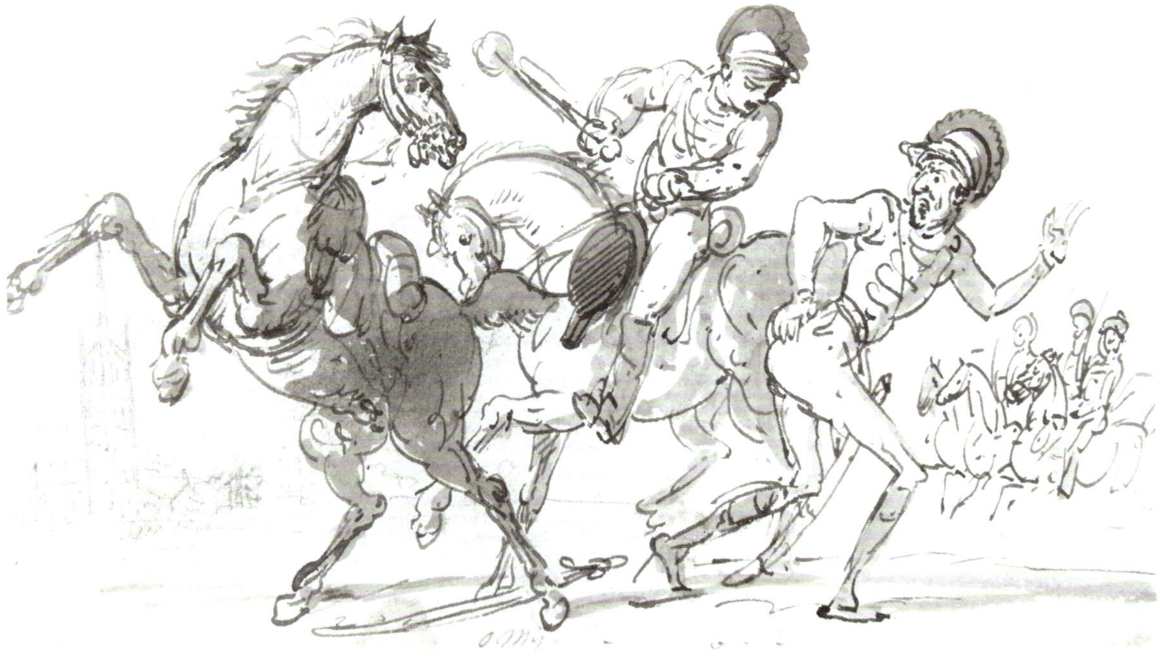

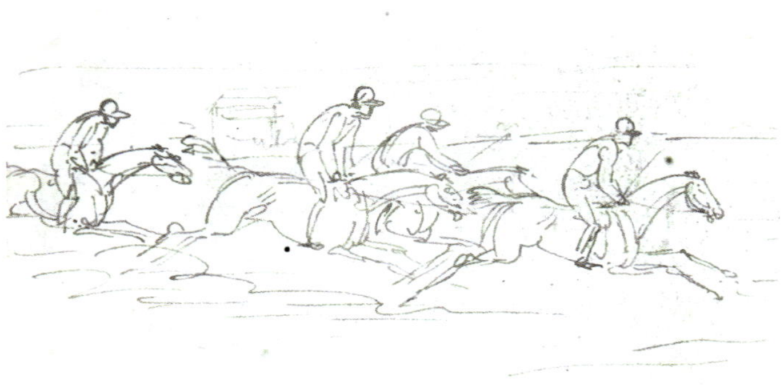

**42** HORSE RACING
*pen and ink*
*3 x 5 ½ inches*



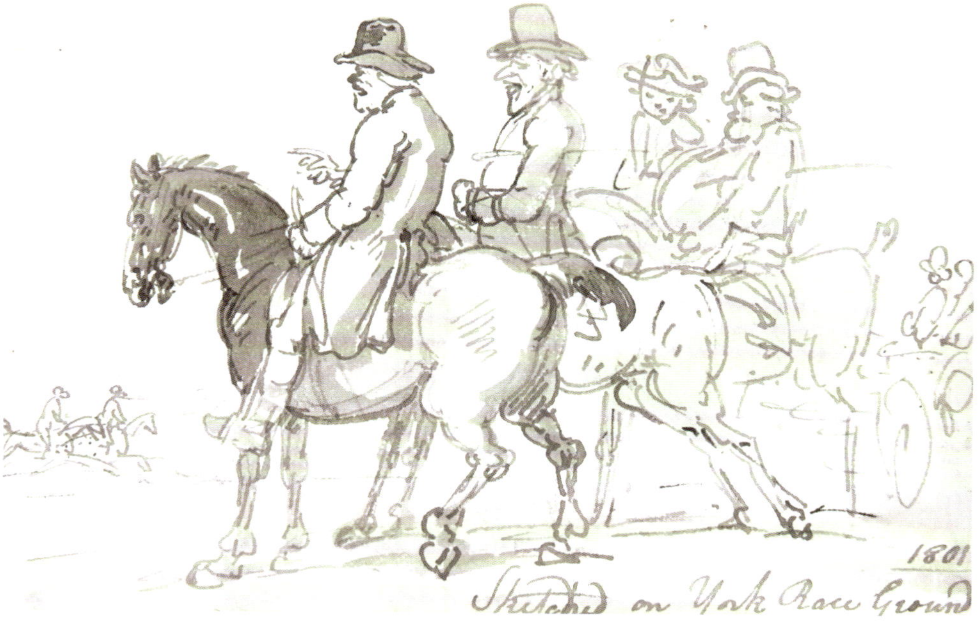


**43** SKETCHED ON YORK RACE GROUND
*inscribed with title and dated 1801*
*pen ink and monochrome watercolour with pencil*
*4 ¼ x 6 ½ inches*

**44** QUARTERLY DUNS, OR CLAMOROUS TAX-GATHERERS (opposite)
*inscribed with title*
*pen ink and watercolour*
*12 ½ x 9 ½ inches*

Provenance: Dr Joseph Chess
Published by Samuel Howitt, 73 Wardour Street, Soho, 1805
Literature: Joseph Grego, *Rowlandson The Caricaturist*, London: Chatto and Windus, 1880, Volume II, page 49
Exhibited: 'Bliss was it in that dawn to be alive, 1750-1850', October 2008, no 63

**Quarterly Duns, or Clamorous Tax-Gatherers**
'Taxation in 1805 raised a great deal of bad feeling; the satirists treated the increased imposts, and the methods of collecting them, from their point of view, and made the public smile at ills to which perforce they were compelled to submit. The house of a quack practitioner in "Rotten Row", one Dr Humbug, at the sign of the Golden Pestle of Hippocrates, who advertises "advice gratis" on his front door, is the scene of a general muster of the inquisitors and collectors of taxes. *Window Tax, Income, Property, House, Servants, Horses, Dogs, &c*, are among the requisitions to be levied. *The Budget opened, or how to raise the wind for the year* 1805 explains these visitations. The quack and his wife are declining to admit their duns; they are surveying the besieging party from an upper window, and the *goodwill* of their house is, according to a placard, *to be disposed of*. The prospect of "Houses to Let" and of windows "Blocked up" shows that taxation was pressing with over-severity, and had, in reality, been carried beyond a joke.'
(Joseph Grego, *Rowlandson the Caricaturist*, London: Chatto and Windus, 1880, Volume II page 49)

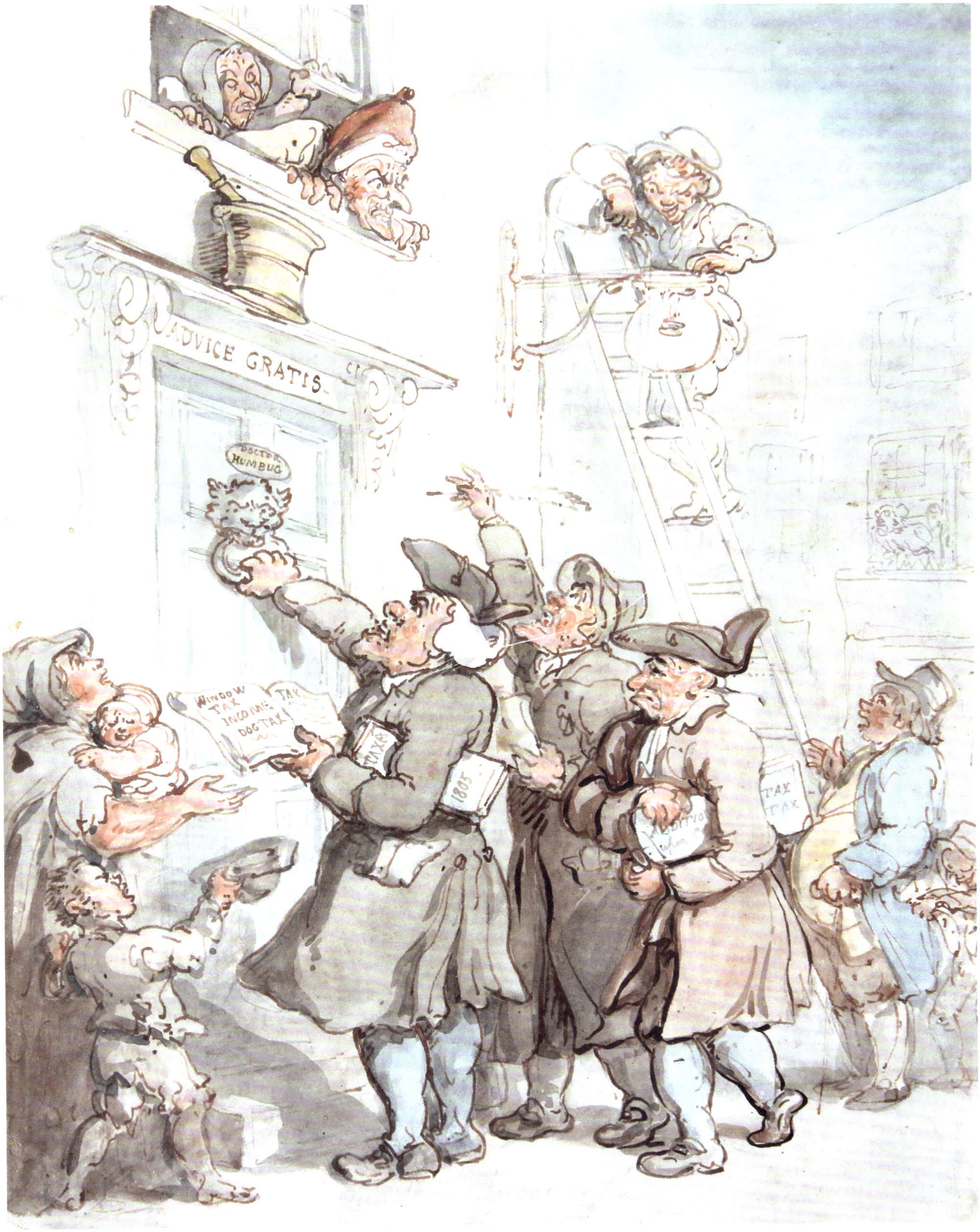
ADVICE GRATIS
DOCTOR HUMBUG
WINDOW TAX
INCOME TAX
DOG TAX
TAX
1805
TAX
TAX

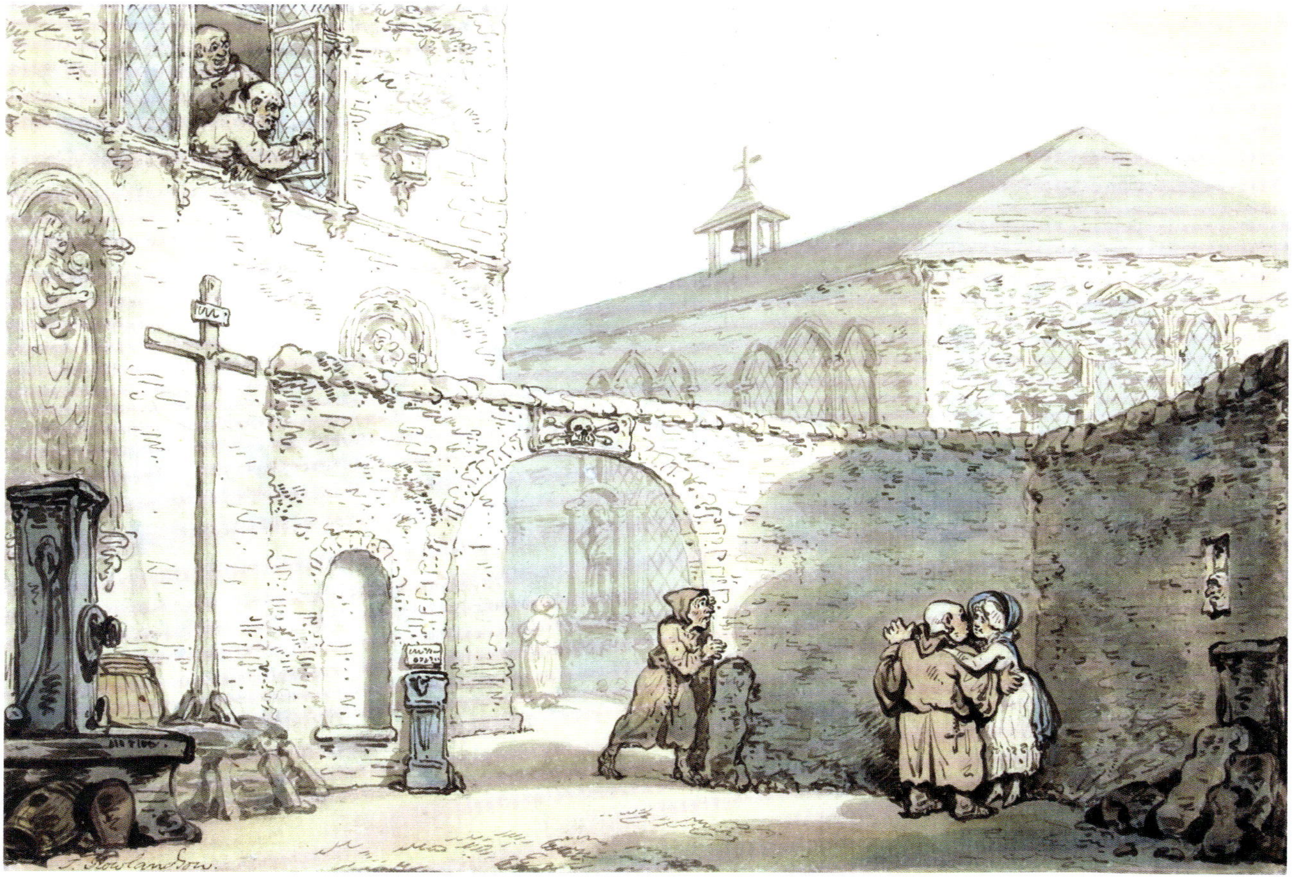



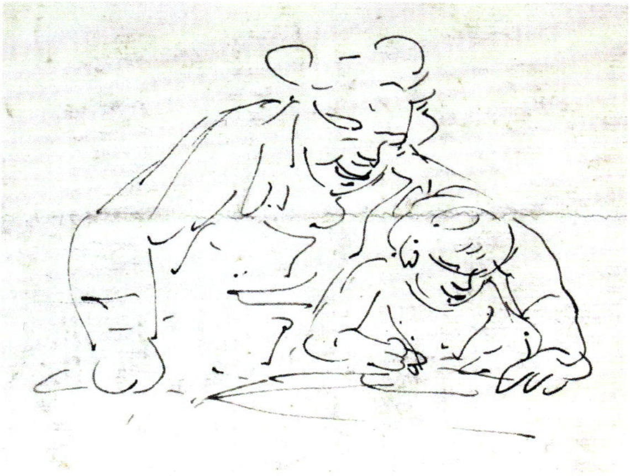

**45** THE COURTYARD OF A MONASTERY
*signed*
*pen ink and watercolour*
*6 ¾ x 9 ¼ inches*

Exhibited: 'Thomas Rowlandson (1756-1827)', Frank T Sabin, 154 New Bond Street, 1933, no 101; Leger Galleries, London, February 1981; 'Bliss was it in that dawn to be alive, 1750-1850', October 2008, no 58

**46** INSTRUCTION – PORTRAITS OF HENRY AND CHARLES
*signed and inscribed with title*
*inscribed 'Saturday Night – Ports Chas + Henry' on reverse*
*pen and ink*
*6 ¼ x 6 ½ inches*
Exhibited: 'Bliss was it in that dawn to be alive, 1750-1850', October 2008

**47** PORTRAIT OF DOCTOR GUISE (opposite)
*inscribed with title*
*pen ink and watercolour*
*11 ¾ x 9 inches*

Provenance: Dr Joseph Chess
Exhibited: 'Bliss was it in that dawn to be alive, 1750-1850', October 2008, no 48

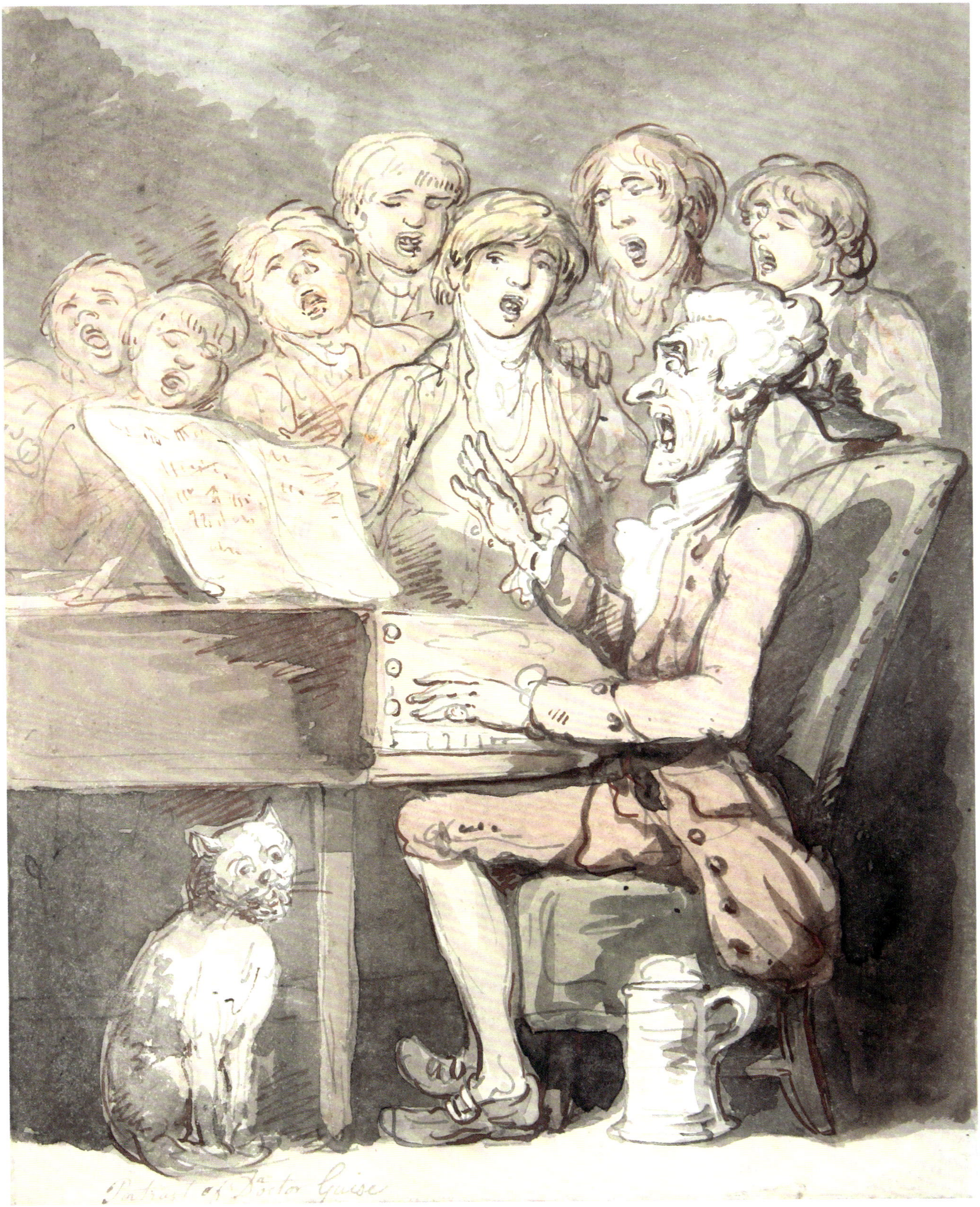

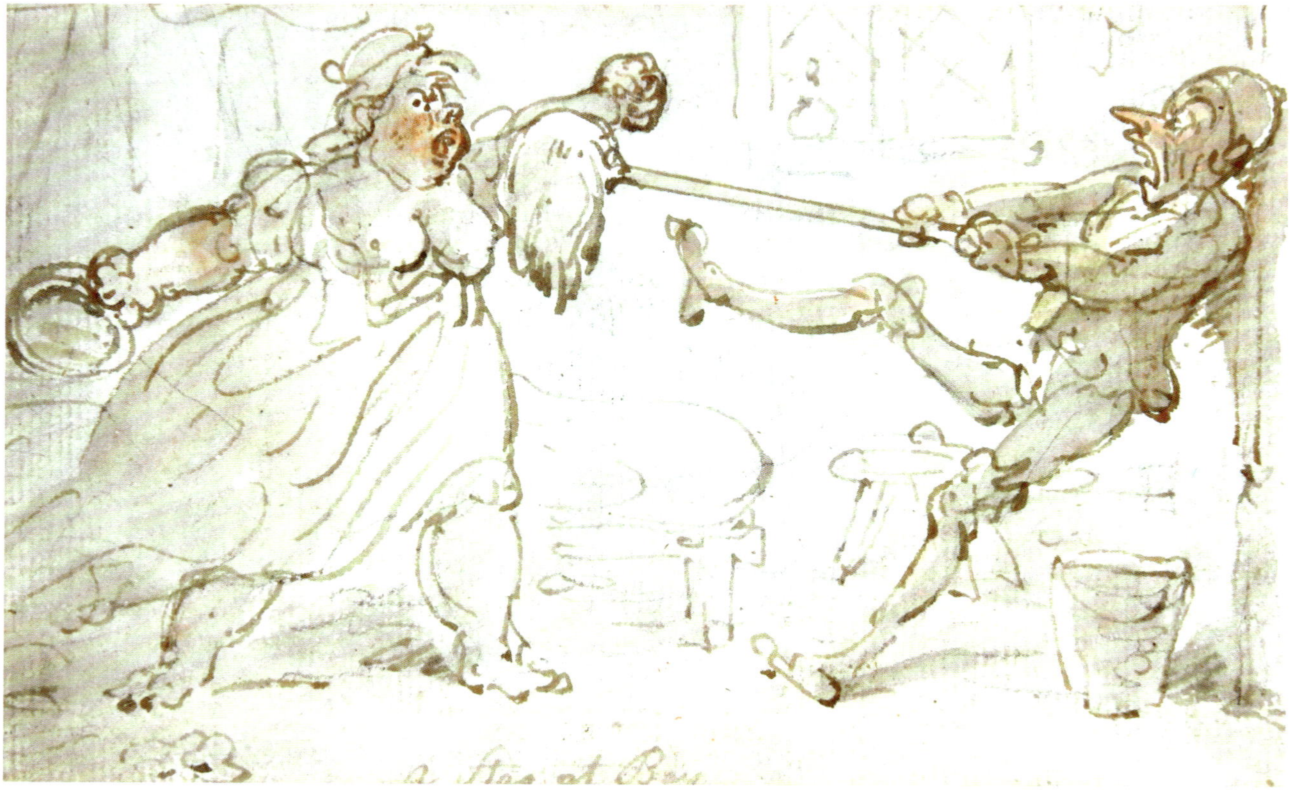



**48** A STAG AT BAY
*inscribed with title*
*pen ink and watercolour with pencil*
*4 x 6 ½ inches*

Reverse:
Buildings
*pencil, 3 ¾ x 6 ¼ inches*

Literature: Joseph Grego, *Rowlandson The Caricaturist*, London: Chatto and Windus, 1880, Volume II, page 120, as *A Stag at Bay, or Conjugal Felicity. A Romance*, dated 1808

**A Stag at Bay**

Rowlandson made a number of drawings with this title, a very similar one being sold at Bonhams Oxford in 2010. They relate to the work listed in Grego as *A Stag at Bay, or Conjugal Felicity. A Romance.* He describes the scene as follows: 'A matrimonial dispute; the wife is attacking her spouse incontinently, and he is protecting himself, and keeping the aggressor at arm's length with a dirty mop'.

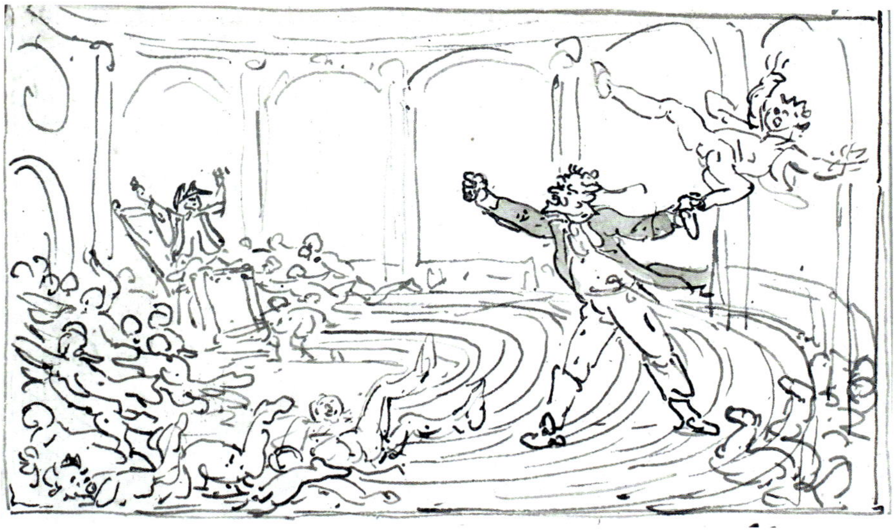

**49** THE BARON MAKES A SPEECH TO THE NATIONAL ASSEMBLY AND DRIVES OUT ALL THE MEMBERS
*inscribed with title*
*pen and ink with watercolour*
*3 ¾ x 5 ¼ inches*

Drawn for but not illustrated in *Surprising adventures of the renowned Baron Munchausen containing singular travels, campaigns, voyages and adventures*, London: Thomas Tegg, 1809
Exhibited: 'Bliss was it in that dawn to be alive, 1750-1850', October 2008, no 64

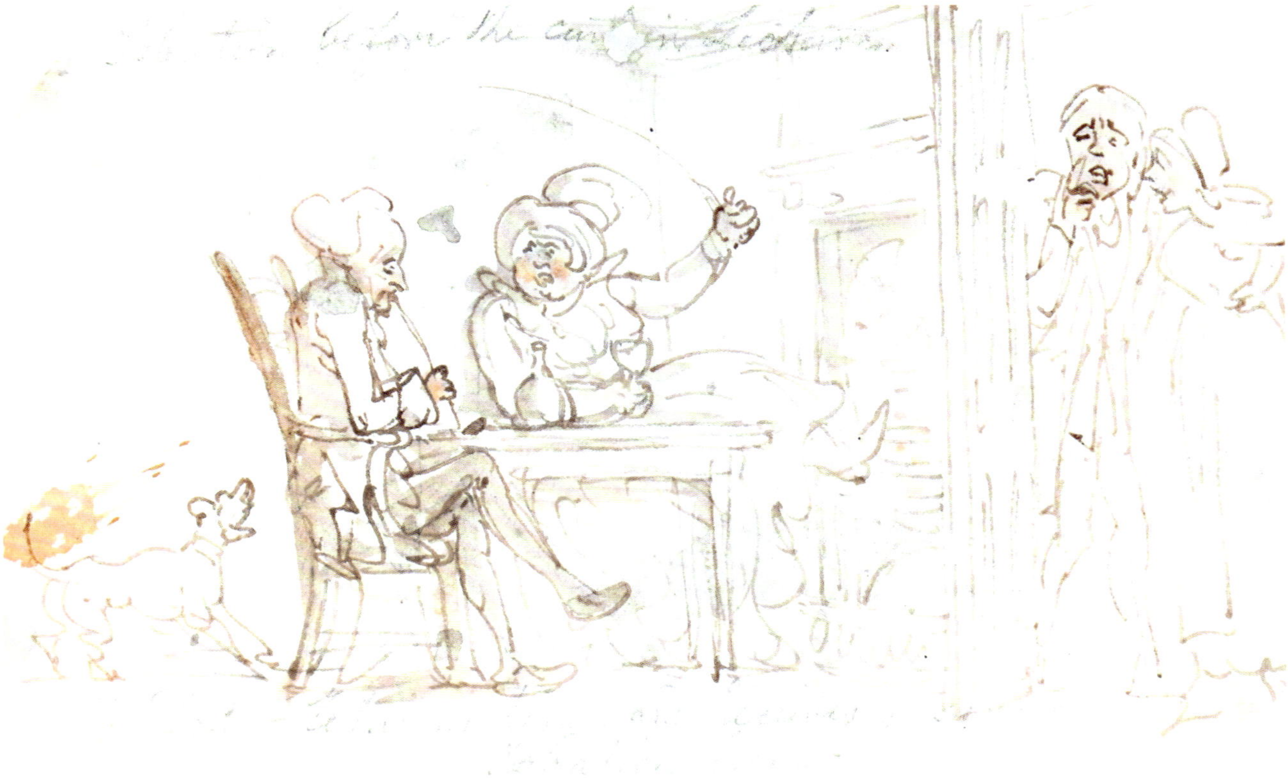



**50** JOBATION BEFORE THE CURTAIN LISTENERS
THE DOCTOR RETURNS HOME AND RECEIVES A SEVERE JOBATION FROM MRS LINGER

*inscribed with title*
*pen ink and watercolour with pencil*
*4 ½ x 7 ½ inches*

Preliminary drawing for William Combe, 'The Schoolmaster's Tour', *Poetical Magazine*, 1809-1811, republished as *The Tour of Dr Syntax in search of the picturesque* in 1812

Literature: Joseph Grego, *Rowlandson The Caricaturist*, London: Chatto and Windus, 1880, Volume II, page 178, as *11. Doctor Syntax returned from his tour* published 1 April 1811

The print that was produced from **50** is illustrated to the right.

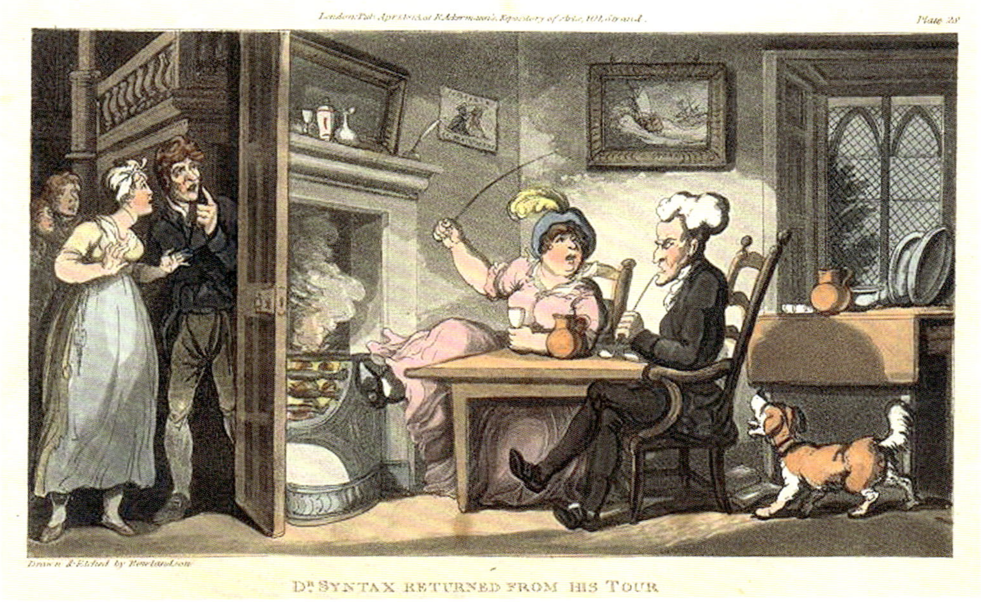

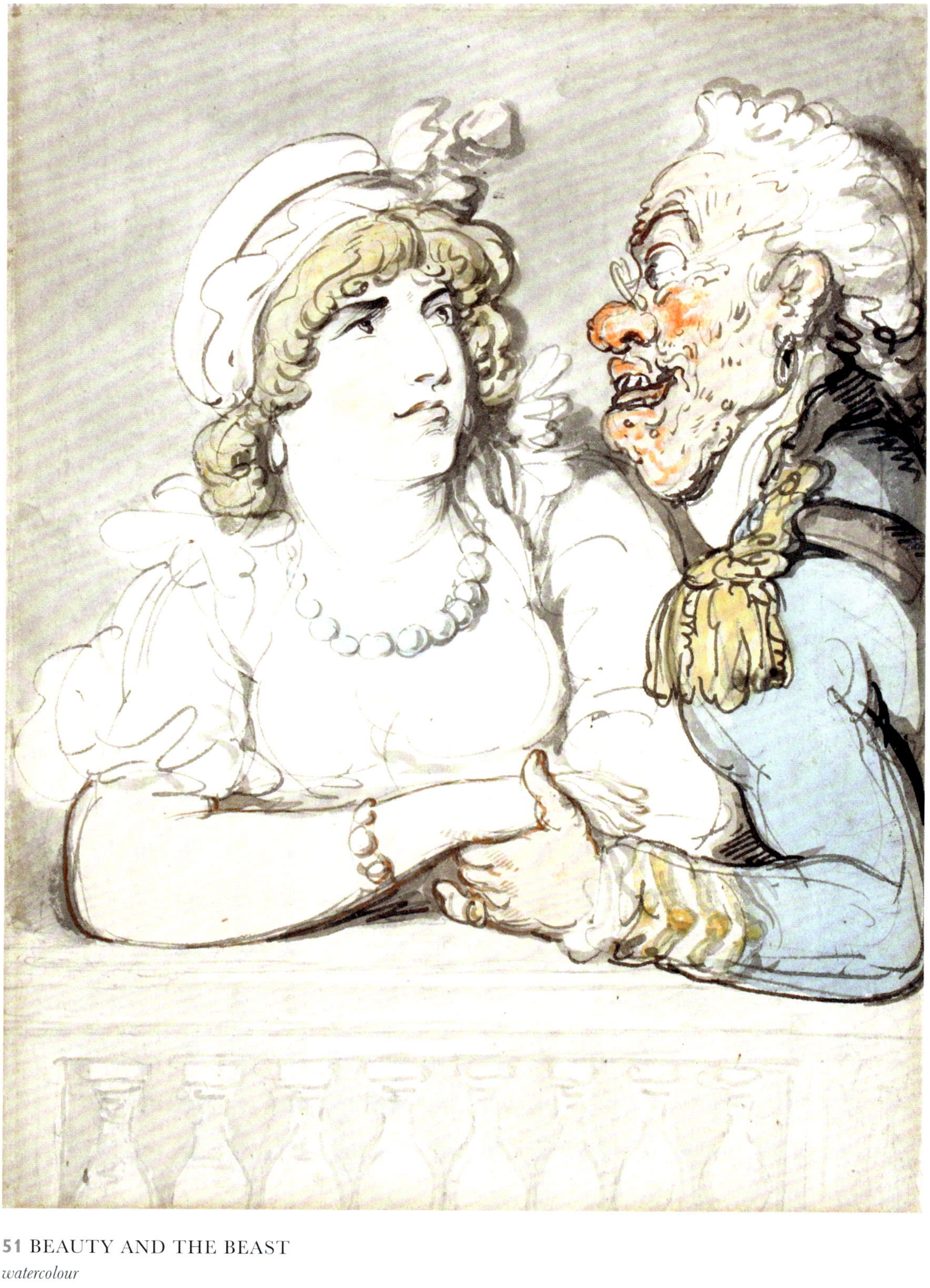

**51** BEAUTY AND THE BEAST
*watercolour*
*10 ¾ x 8 inches*

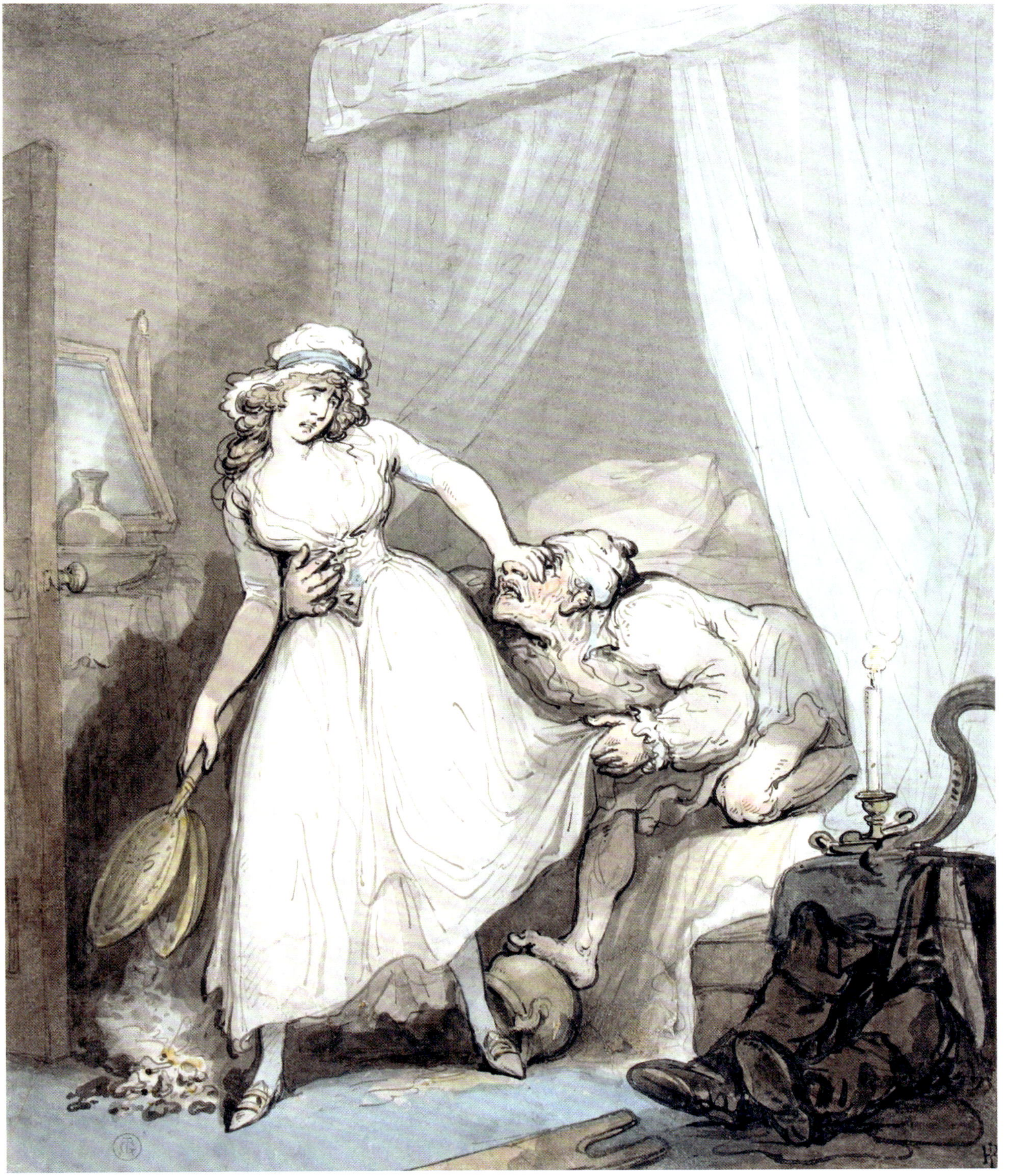



**52** THE VIRTUOUS CHAMBERMAID
*inscribed with monogram 'HB' and stamped with monogram 'JG'*
*pen ink and watercolour*
*11 x 9 inches*

Provenance: The Reitlinger Collection
Literature: John Hayes, *The Art of Thomas Rowlandson*, Alexandria, VA: Art Services International, 1990, page 46
Exhibited: Leger Galleries, London, February 1981, no 50; 'Bliss was it in that dawn to be alive, 1750-1850', October 2008, no 35

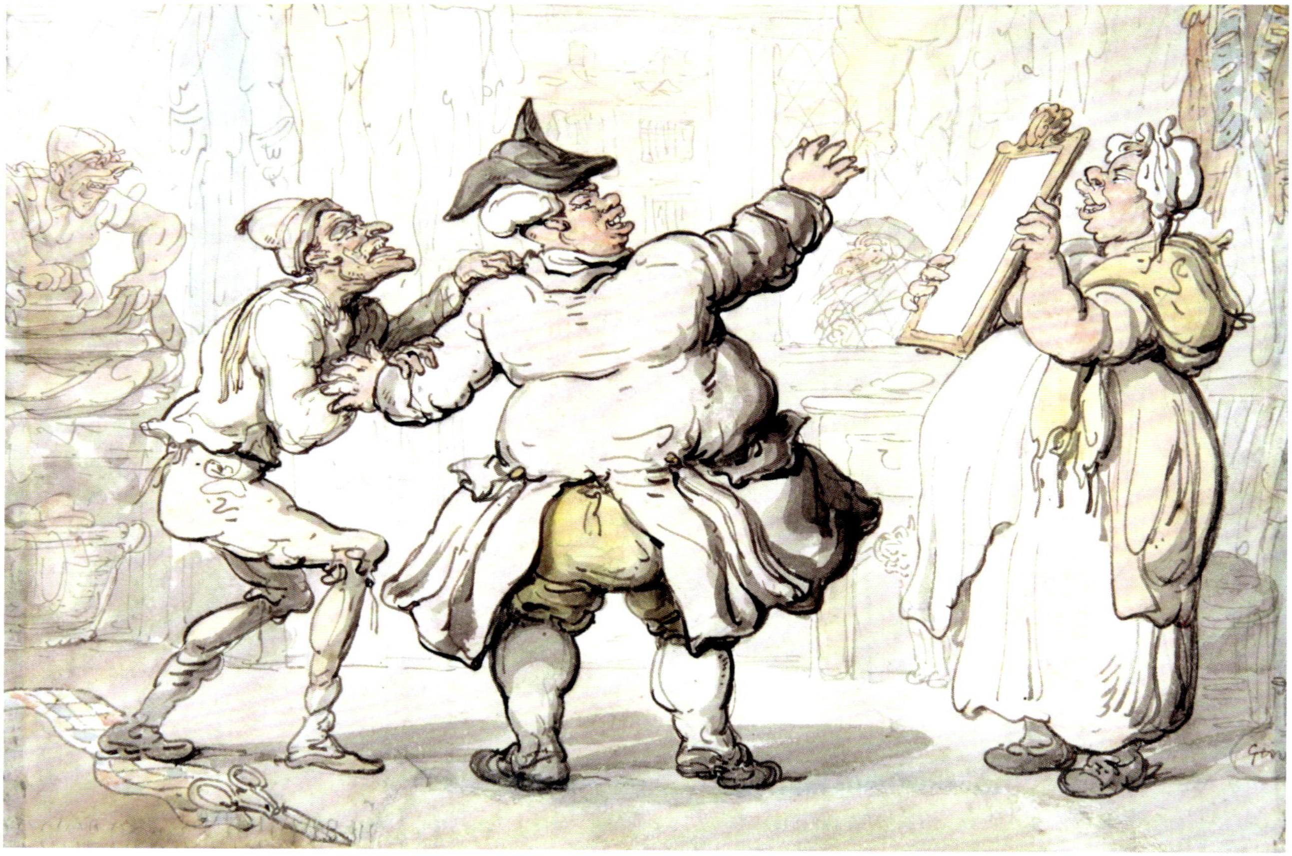



**53** AT THE TAILOR'S
*pen ink and watercolour*
*7 ¼ x 10 ½ inches*

Exhibited: 'Bliss was it in that dawn to be alive, 1750-1850', October 2008, no 68

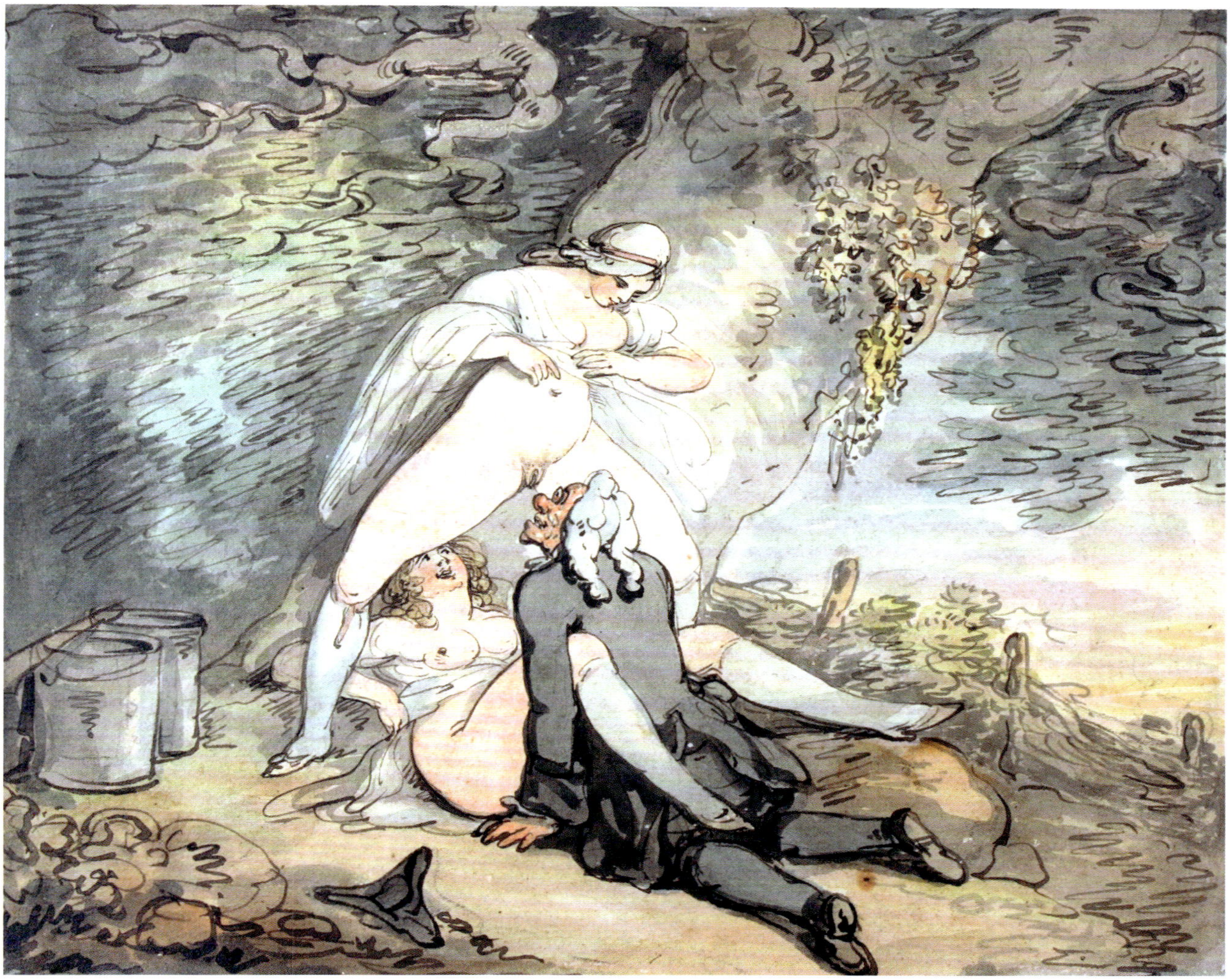



**54** THE PARSON AND THE MILKMAIDS
*watercolour*
*7 x 8 ½ inches*

Provenance: Spink Leger
Exhibited: 'Bliss was it in that dawn to be alive, 1750-1850',
October 2008, no 78

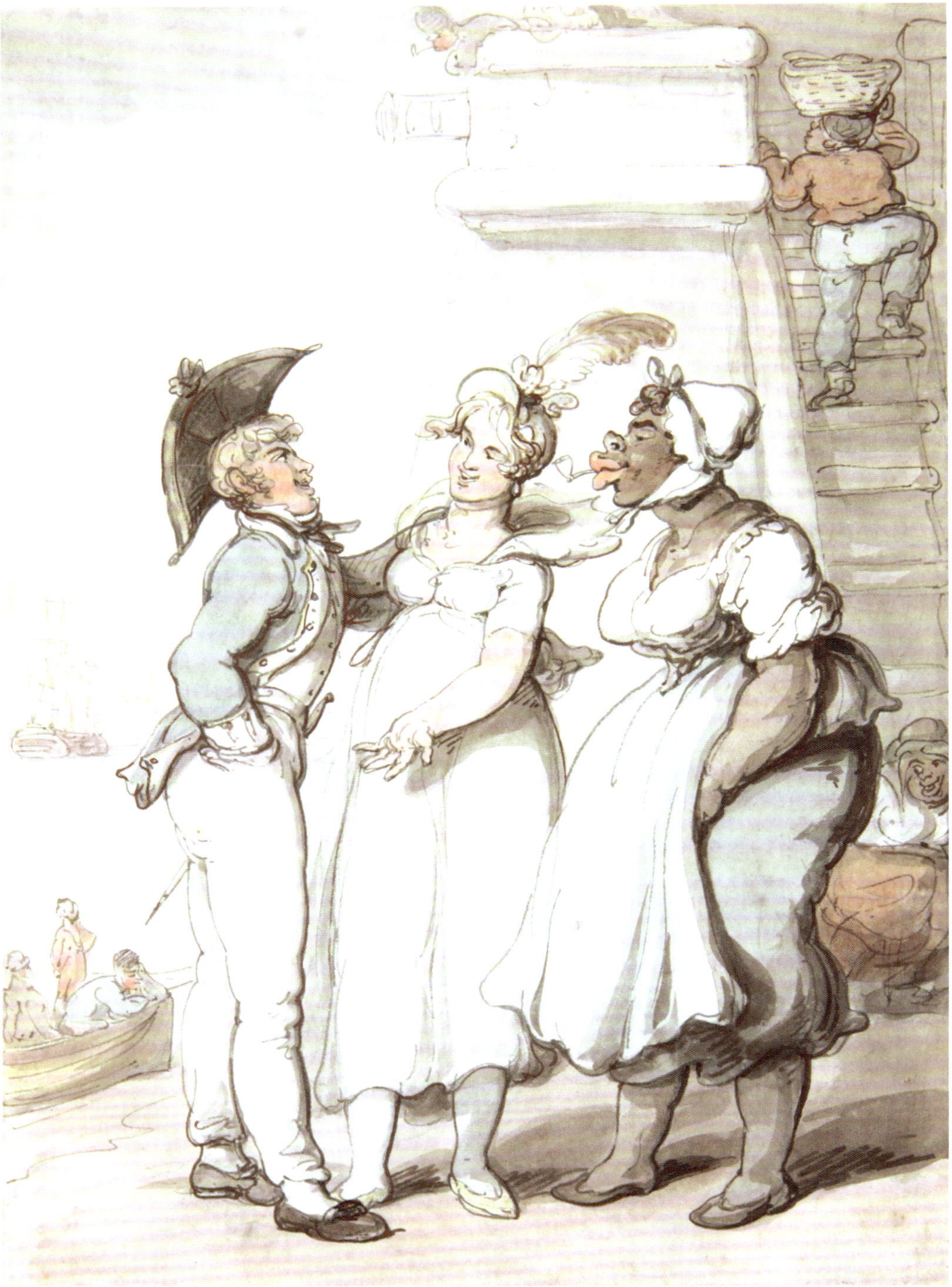



**55** SEA STORES

*pen ink and watercolour, 13 ¼ x 9 ½ inches*

Published, in reverse, by Thomas Tegg, 25 March 1812, as a pair with *Land Stores*
Literature: Joseph Grego, *Rowlandson The Caricaturist*, London: Chatto and Windus, 1880, Volume II, page 226; Mary Dorothy George, *Catalogue of Political and Personal Satires*, no 11960
Exhibited: 'Bliss was it in that dawn to be alive, 1750-1850', October 2008, no 76

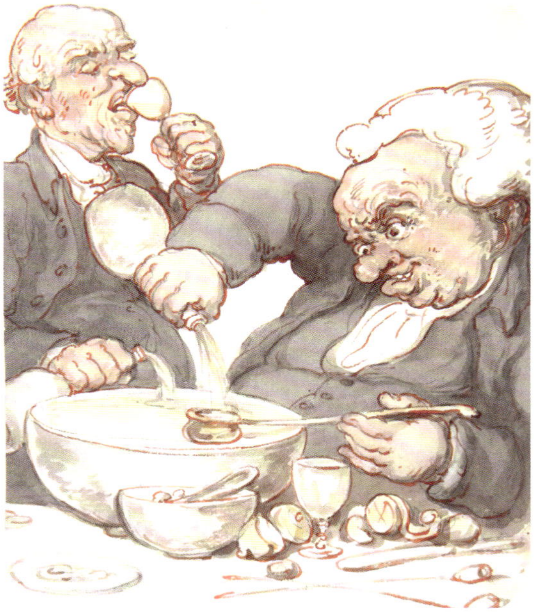

57 MIXING THE PUNCH
*pen ink and watercolour with pencil*
*8 ¼ x 6 ¾ inches*



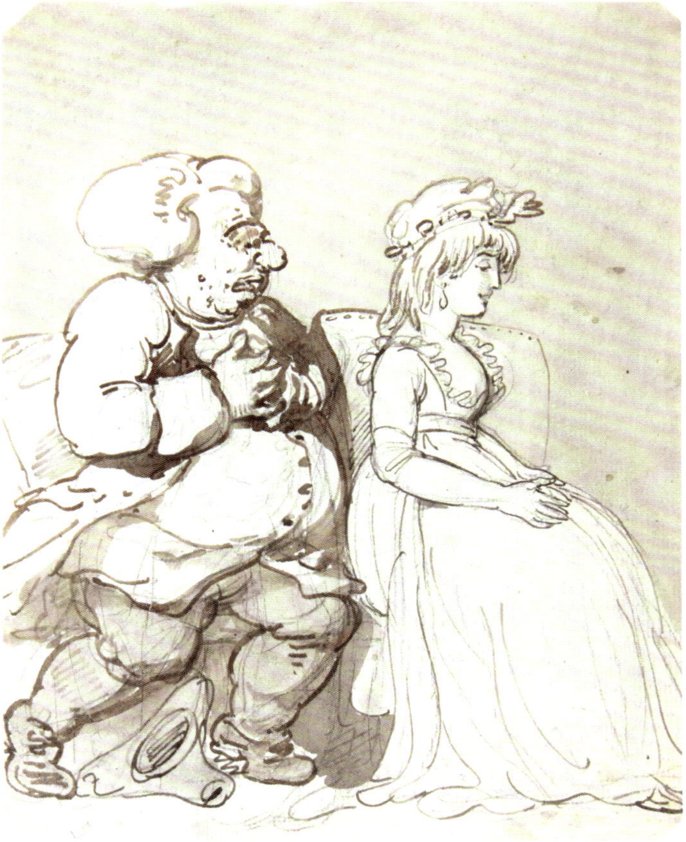

56 ROMANTIC OVERTURES
*monochrome watercolour with pencil*
*9 ¼ x 7 ¼ inches*

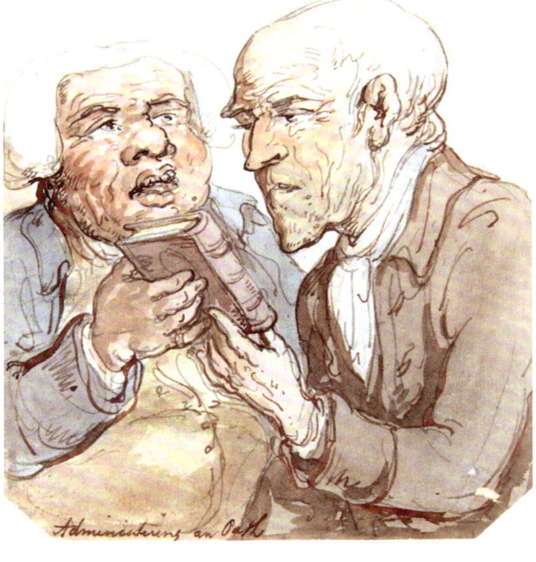


58 ADMINISTERING AN OATH
*inscribed with title and 'Bribery & Corruption'*
*pen ink and watercolour with pencil*
*7 ½ x 6 ¼ inches*

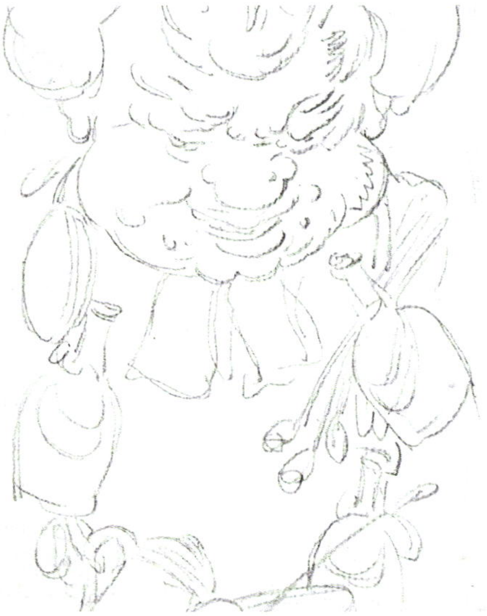

**59** PARSON'S PLEASURE
*pencil*
*5 x 4 inches*

Exhibited: 'Bliss was it in that dawn to be alive, 1750-1850', October 2008, no 69

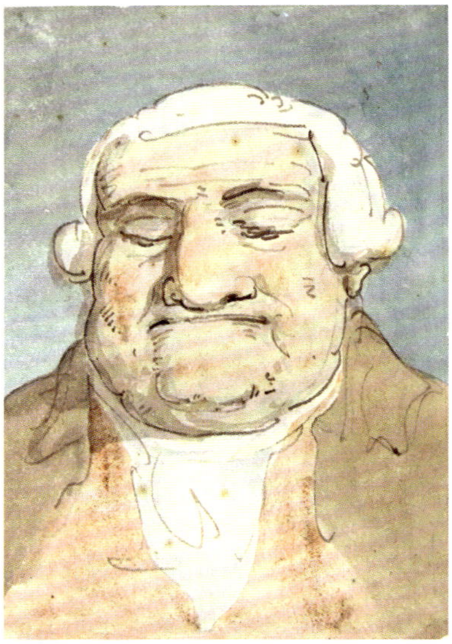

**60** HALF ASLEEP
*pen ink and watercolour with pencil*
*7 x 5 inches*



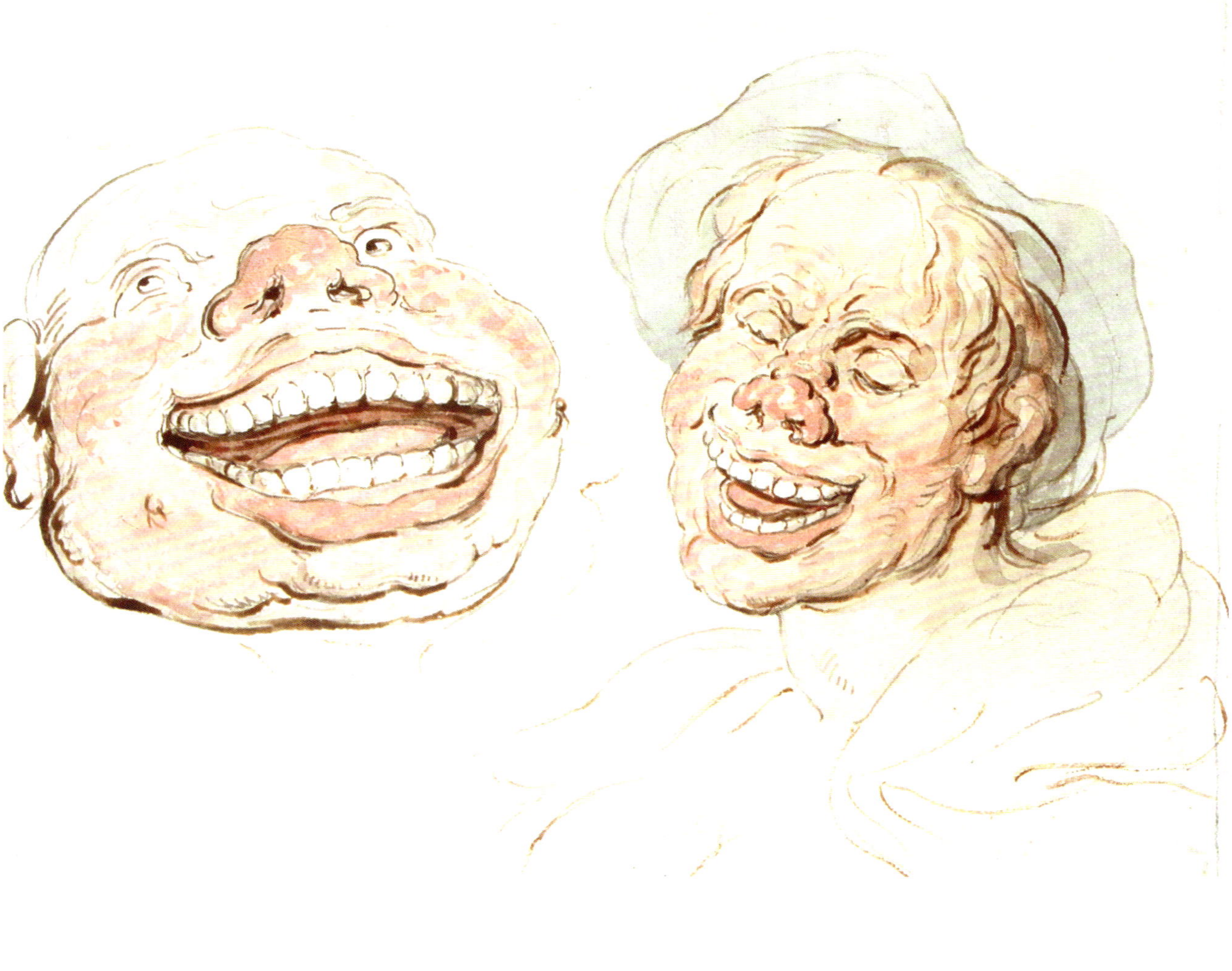

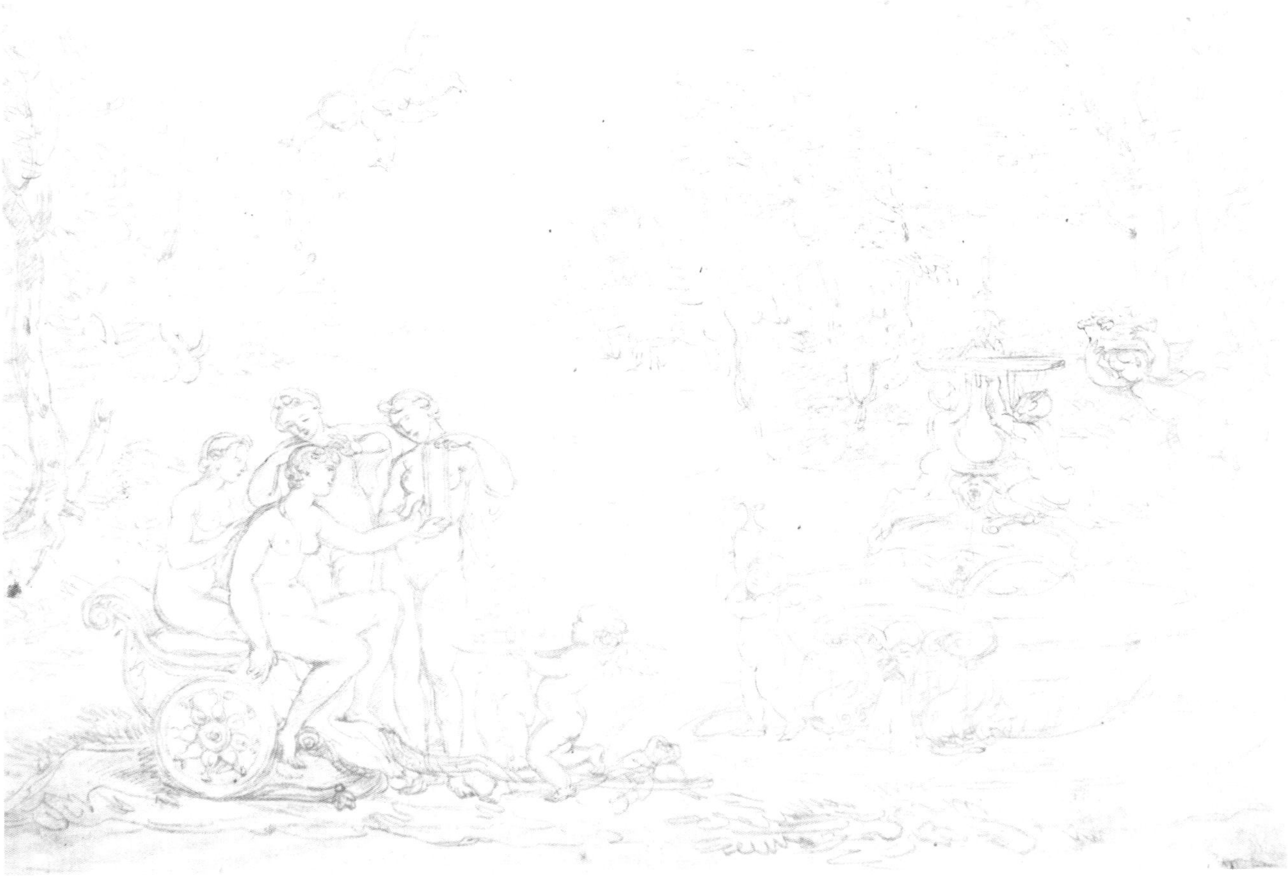



**62** THE CAR OF VENUS
*pencil*
*7 x 9 ¾ inches*

**61** LAUGHING GROTESQUES (opposite)
*pen ink and watercolour*
*5 x 6 ¾ inches*

Exhibited: 'Bliss was it in that dawn to be alive, 1750-1850', October 2008, no 75

**63** THE INTRUDER
*pencil*
*7 ½ x 5 ½ inches*

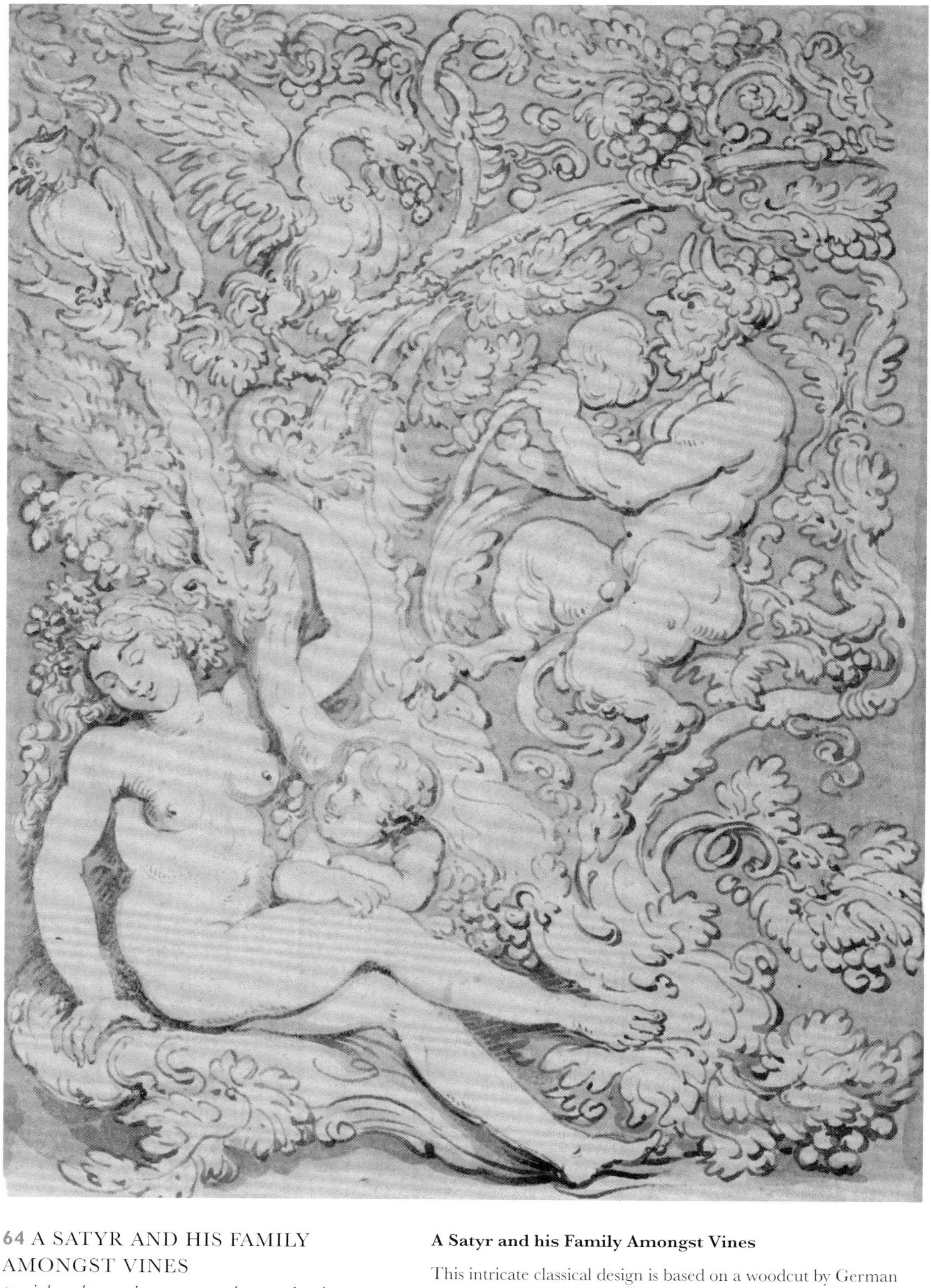



**64** A SATYR AND HIS FAMILY AMONGST VINES

*pen ink and monochrome watercolour on tinted paper*

*8 ½ x 6 ¼ inches*

**A Satyr and his Family Amongst Vines**

This intricate classical design is based on a woodcut by German printmaker Sebald Beham (1500-1550). Beham worked as an engraver, glass painter, woodcut designer and illustrator in Nuremburg in the first part of the sixteenth century. Repeated prints of the original woodcut were used for wallpaper designs in Nuremburg around 1520-25 and there is one such design in the collection of the British Museum.

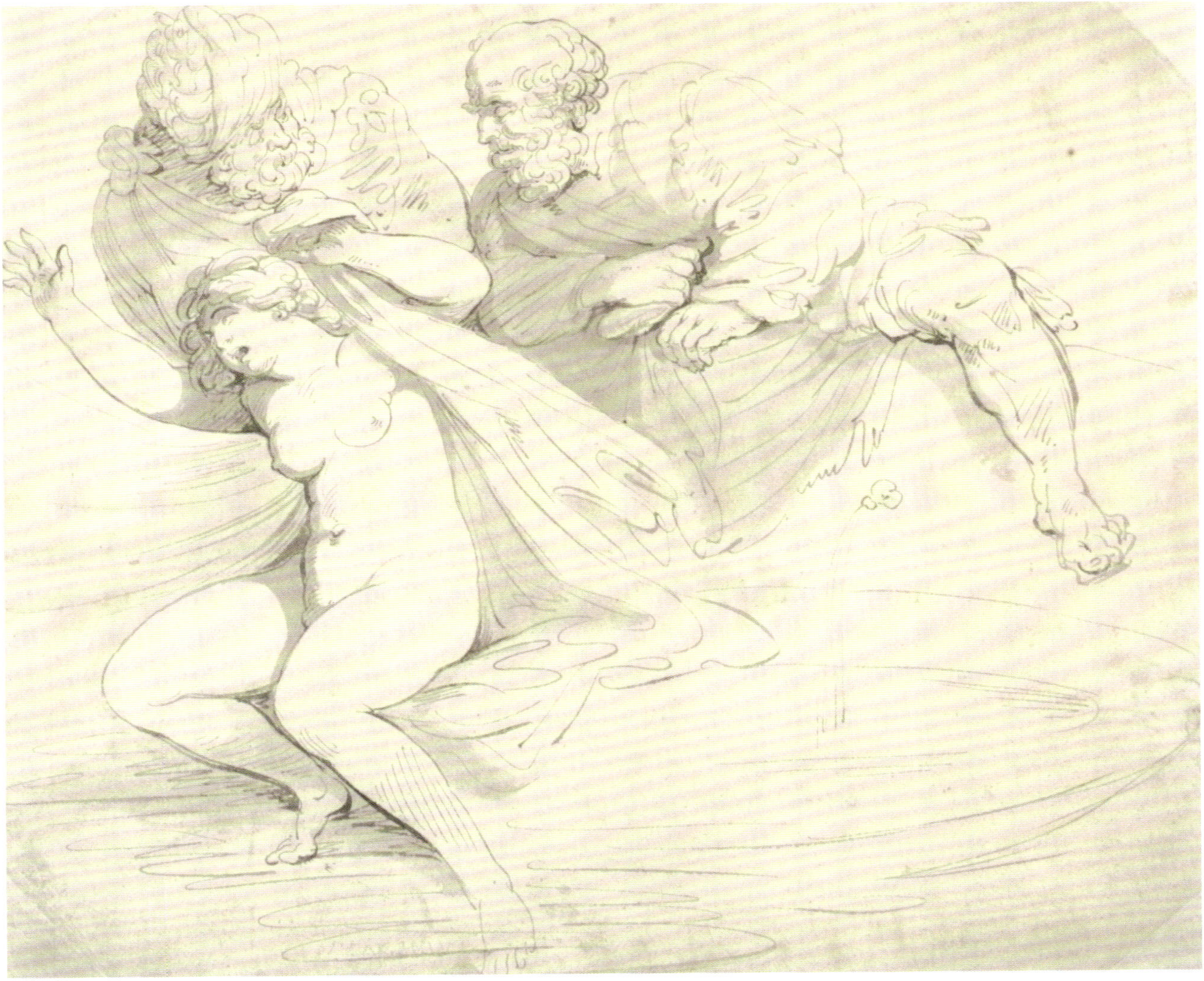



**65** SUSANNAH AND THE ELDERS

*pen ink and monochrome watercolour*

*9 ¼ x 11 inches*

Provenance: W Coleman Collection; Sabin Galleries, May 1964
Exhibited: 'Bliss was it in that dawn to be alive, 1750-1850', October 2008, no 66

**Susannah and The Elders**

Rowlandson made a number of studies based on, or influenced by, the paintings of Old Masters. These drawings took the form of classical figure studies and were often erotic in theme, giving Rowlandson the chance to indulge in one of his favourite pastimes, the glorification of the naked female form.

Grego lists a drawing by Rowlandson – based on a painting of this subject by Guercino – as being in the collection of Colonel Gould Weston, Thurloe Square (Volume II, page 427). It tells the story of Susannah, from the Book of Daniel, who was falsely accused of adultery. While bathing naked in her garden, she is observed by two elderly voyeurs, who covet her youth and beauty. They accost her and threaten to claim that she was meeting a young man, unless she agrees to sleep with them. However, Susannah refuses to be blackmailed and is arrested. Just as she is about to be executed for her crimes, a man named Daniel intervenes on her behalf, and the old men are questioned. When their stories fail to match up, Susannah's innocence is proven and the false accusers are put to death instead.

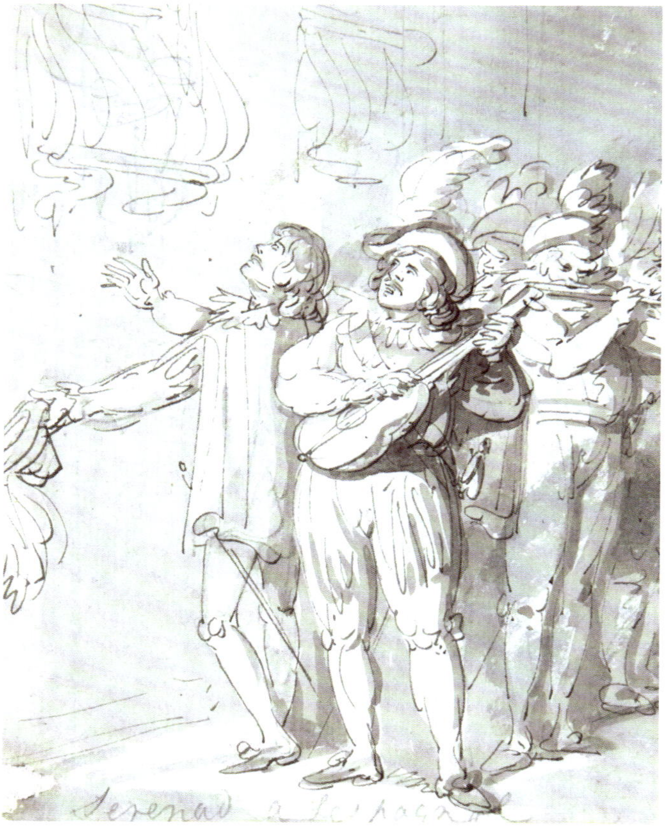

**66** SERENADE
*inscribed 'Serenad a Lespagnol'*
*pen ink and watercolour with pencil*
*6 ¼ x 4 ¾ inches*

**67** THE COQUETTE
'I'LL LEAD YOU TO THE SPLENDID CROWD
BUT YOUR NEXT DRESS WILL BE A SHROUD'
*signed*
*pen ink and watercolour*
*4 ½ x 8 inches*

Similar to *The Coquette*, published by Rudolph Ackermann for *The English Dance of Death*, 1 October 1814, plate 21
Literature: Joseph Grego, *Rowlandson The Caricaturist*, London: Chatto and Windus, 1880, Volume II, page 331
Exhibited: 'Bliss was it in that dawn to be alive, 1750-1850', October 2008, no 77



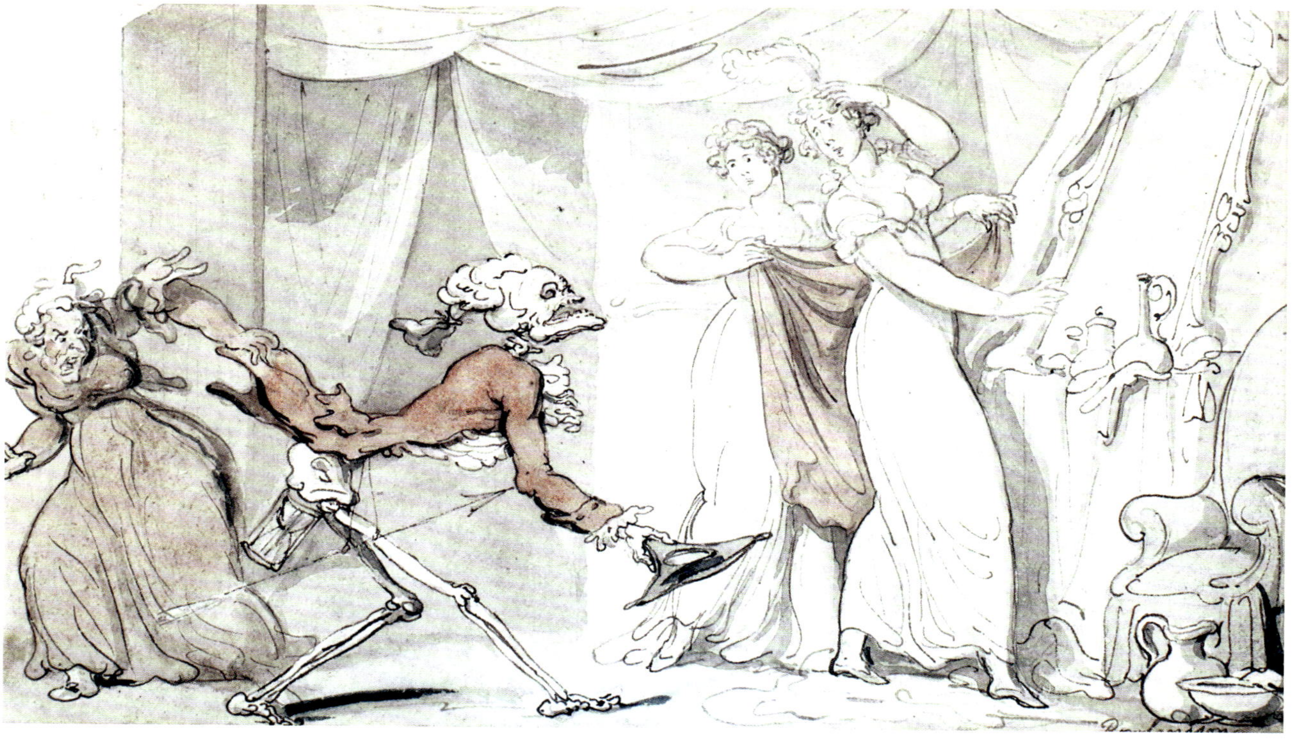

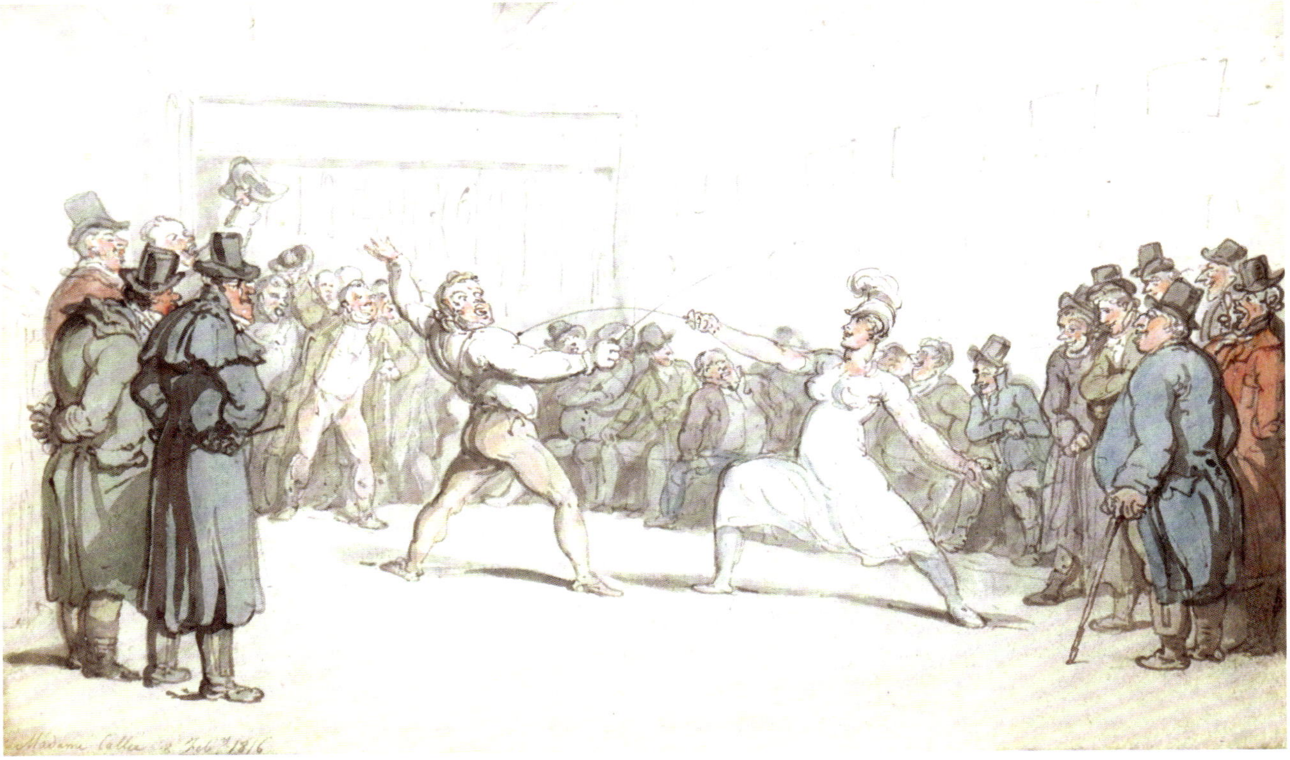



**68** MADAME CALLEE (CULLONI) AND M RENAULT IN A FENCING CONTEST

*inscribed 'Madame Callee' and dated '8th Feb 1816'*
*pen ink and watercolour*
*6 x 9 ½ inches*

Exhibited: 'Bliss was it in that dawn to be alive, 1750-1850', October 2008, no 81

**Madame Callee (Culloni) and M Renault in a Fencing Contest**

In about 1785, Henry Angelo inherited from his father the leading London fencing academy, and moved it from Carlisle House, Soho, to the Opera House Buildings, Haymarket. Following a fire at the premises on 17 June 1789, he moved again to 13 Bond Street. Then, in 1795, he began to share the address with his friend, John Jackson (1769-1845), who ran a boxing academy. Also a friend of Rowlandson, who was an amateur fencer and boxer, Angelo commissioned the artist to produce 24 plates illustrating *Hungarian and Highland Broad Sword*, in 1798 [see **05**]. Later in life, he published his *Reminiscences* (1828) – in which he remembers Rowlandson – and *Angelo's Pic-Nic* (1834). By that time, the academy had moved to 32 St James's Street, and was headed by Henry Charles Angelo (1780-1852), Angelo's second son.

During the period that Angelo ran his fencing academy, Rowlandson produced a number of drawings and engravings of fencing matches. Notable among these is a series of at least nine different images showing a display match involving an Italian woman fencer. The present drawing is one of these. The woman, who has never been properly identified but is thought to be a 'Native of Rome', is given a slightly different name in almost every version: Cain, Callee, Collie, Culleoni, Culloni, Cullu, Kelu. While the compositions are all very similar, some are inscribed as 'Angelo's Academy' and others 'Grand Assault, Paris', while the combatant is either a 'Mons Renault' or Angelo himself.

Three are dated to 8 February 1816, including the present drawing and the version illustrated in Angelo's *Reminiscences*, which locates the event to Bond Street. However, the finished version that is closest to the present drawing (that illustrated in V P Sabin, 1933, page 37) is inscribed 'Madame Culloni and Mons Renault, Grand Assault, Paris'. They are both based on an outline drawing in the Huntington Collection. Clearly Culloni and Renault could not have been in London and Paris at the same time, so what seems like documentary evidence may, after all, be artistic licence. **DW**

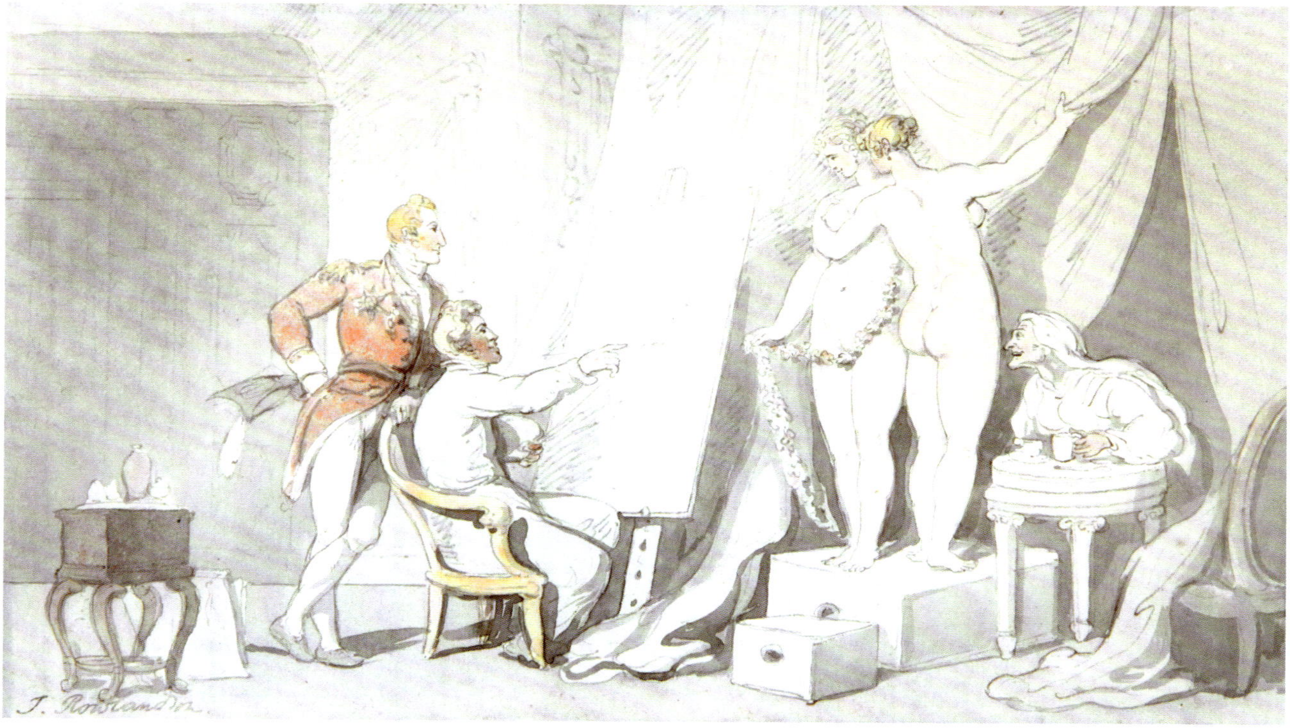


**69** DRAWING FROM LIFE
*signed*
*pen ink and watercolour with pencil*
*5 ¾ x 9 ½ inches*

Possibly drawn for but not illustrated in Bernard Blackmantle [Charles Molloy Westmacott], *The English Spy*, London: Sherwood, Jones & Co, 1825-26 (2 volumes)
Exhibited: 'Bliss was it in that dawn to be alive, 1750-1850', October 2008, no 80

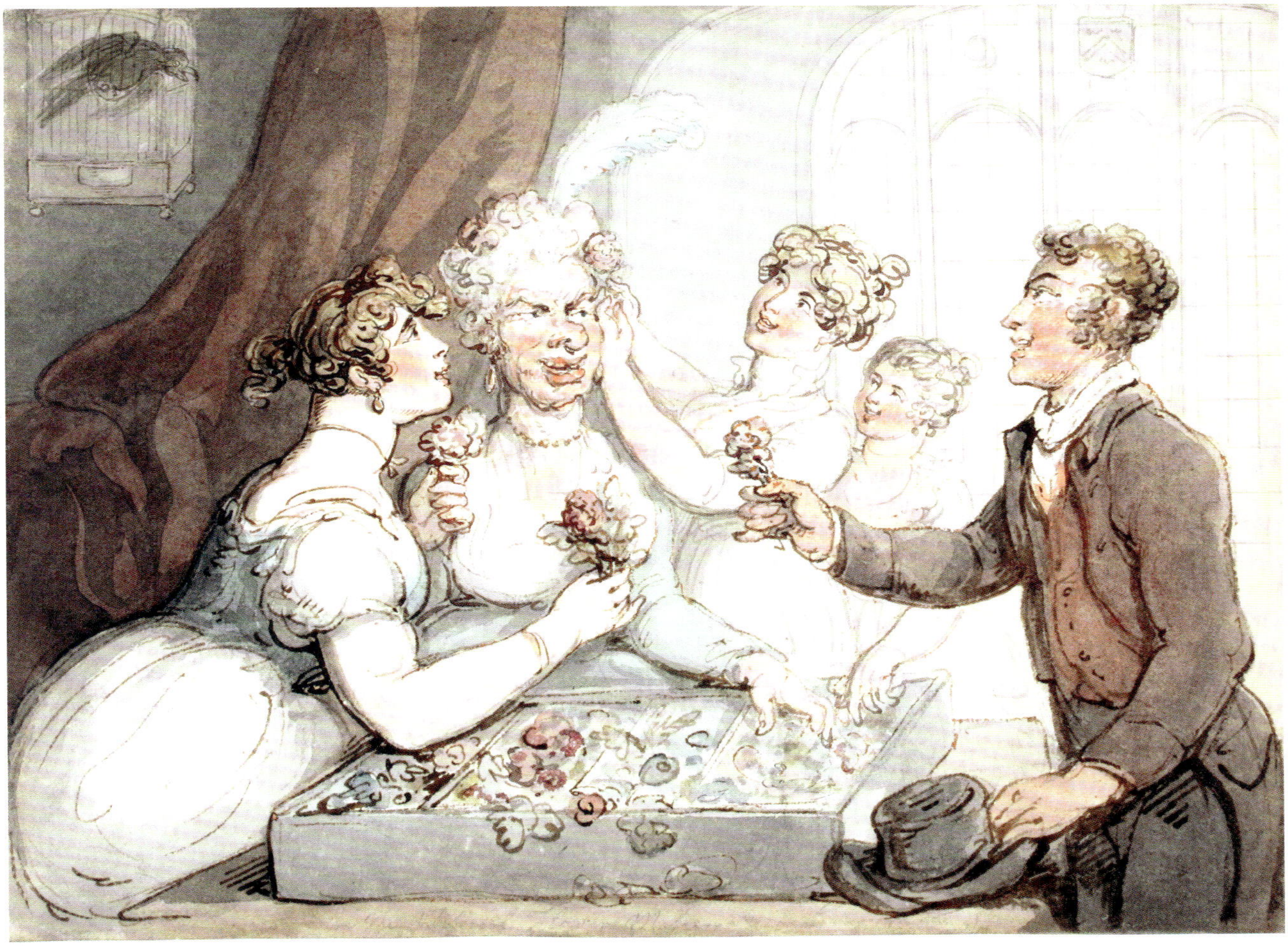



**70** THE ARTIFICIAL FLOWER MAKERS
*inscribed with title*
*watercolour*
*8 ½ x 11 inches*

Exhibited: 'Bliss was it in that dawn to be alive, 1750-1850', October 2008, no 79

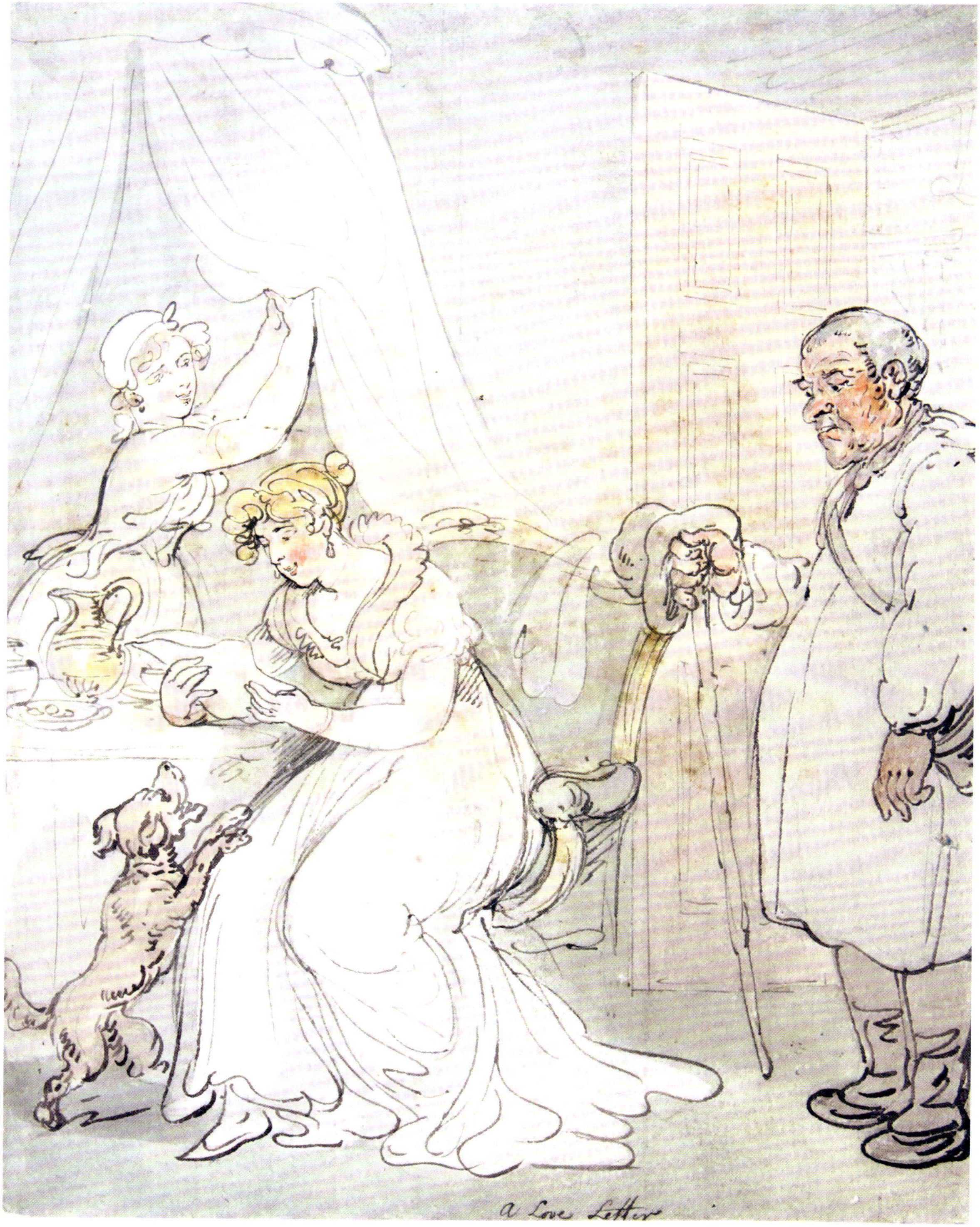




**71** A LOVE LETTER
*inscribed with title*
*pen ink and watercolour*
*11 x 8 ¼ inches*

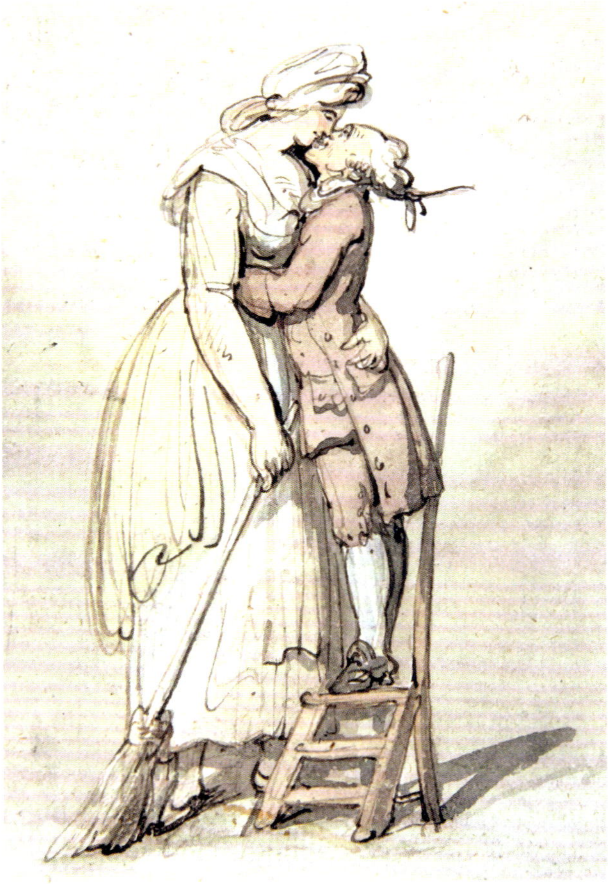

**72** A LITTLE HELP IN KISSING THE MAID
*pen ink and watercolour*
*6 x 4 ¼ inches*

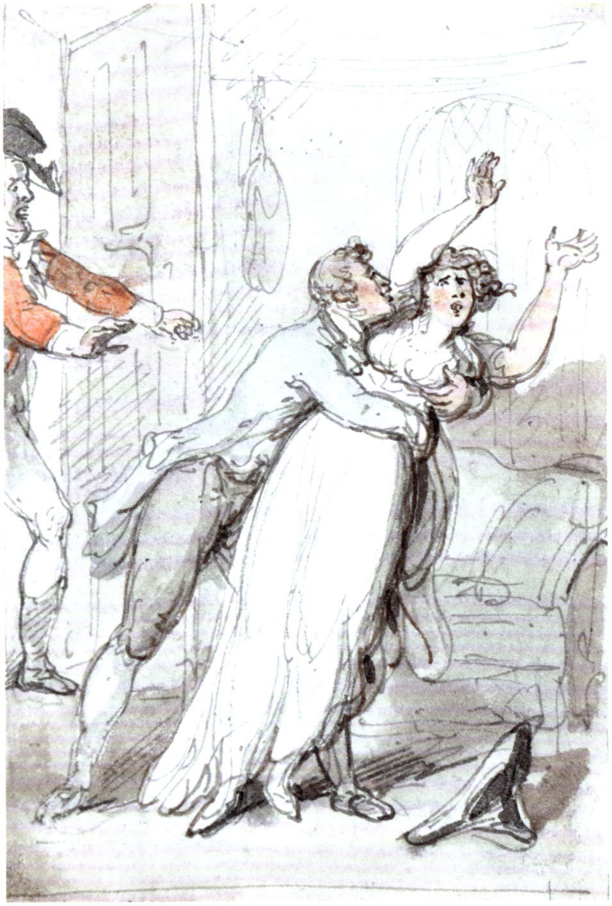

**73** INFIDELITY DISCOVERED
*pen ink and watercolour with pencil*
*5 ½ x 4 inches*

Provenance: Leger Gallery

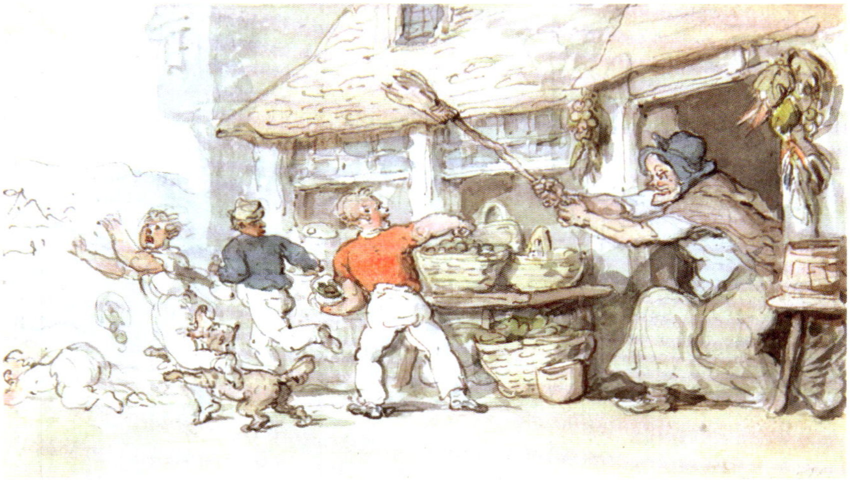

**74** THIEVES
*pen ink and watercolour with pencil*
*3 ¼ x 5 ½ inches*

Reverse:
A chronological list of Kings and Queens of England from Edward VII to George III, dated 1826



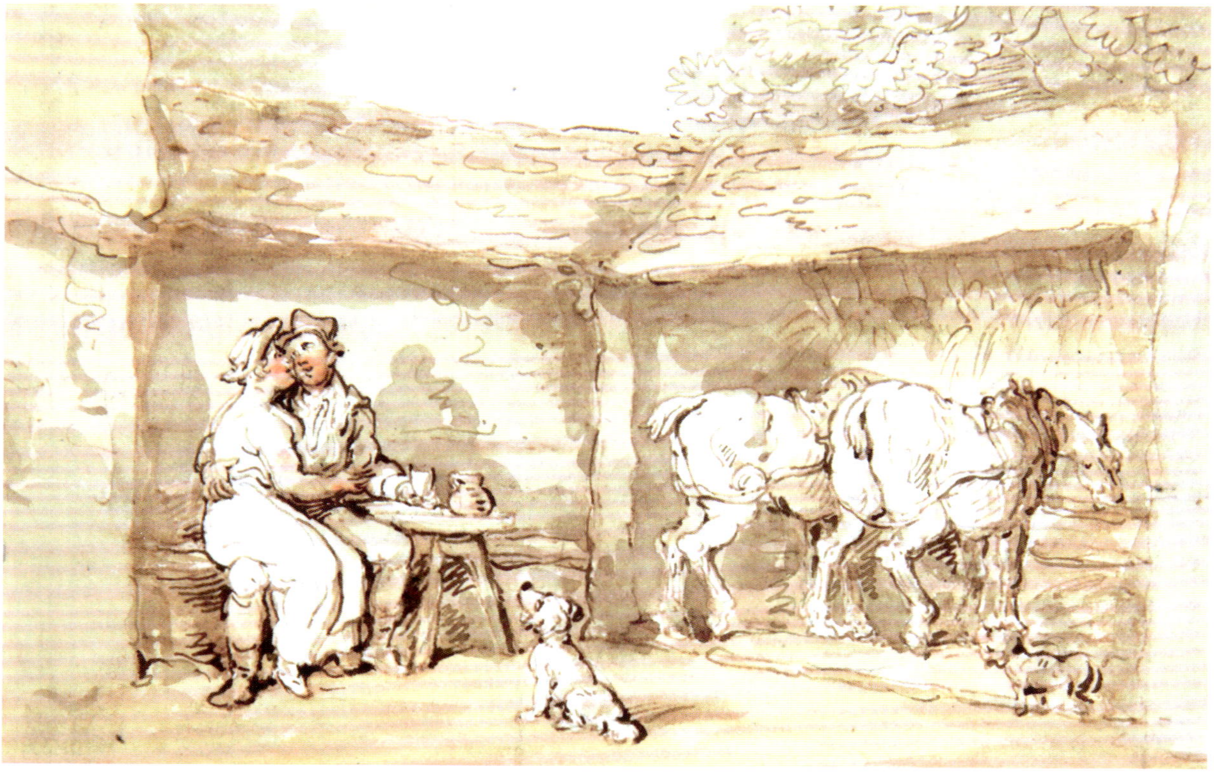

**75** COURTING CARTER
*drawn on reverse of an envelope addressed to the artist at 'Bryan, Blackheath Vale, Blackheath' and post marked '3 Ju'*
*pen ink and watercolour with pencil*
*4 x 6 ¼ inches*

# SELECT BIBLIOGRAPHY


**Bury 1973**
Adrian Bury, *Rowlandson Drawings*, London: Avalon Press, 1973

**Falk 1949**
Bernard Falk, *Thomas Rowlandson: His Art and Life*, London: Hutchinson & Co, 1949

**Grego 1880**
Joseph Grego, *Rowlandson The Caricaturist*, London: Chatto and Windus, 1880 (2 Volumes)

**Hayes 1972**
John Hayes, *Rowlandson: Watercolours and Drawings*, London: Phaidon Press, 1972

**Hayes 1990**
John Hayes, *The Art of Thomas Rowlandson*, Alexandria, VA: Art Services International, 1990

**Hayes 2004**
John Hayes, 'Rowlandson, Thomas (1757-1827)', in H C G Matthew and Brian Harrison (eds), *Oxford Dictionary of National Biography*, Oxford University Press, 2004, Volume 48, pages 13-16

**Heintzelman 1947**
Arthur W Heintzelman, *The Watercolor Drawings of Thomas Rowlandson. From the Albert H Wiggin Collection in the Boston Public Library*, New York: Watson-Guptill Publications, 1947

**Libson 2007**
Lowell Libson (ed), *Beauty and the Beast. A Loan Exhibition of Rowlandson's Works from British Private Collections*, London: Lowell Libson, 2007

**Paulson 1972**
Ronald Paulson, *Rowlandson. A new interpretation*, London: Studio Vista, 1972

**Phagan 2011**
Patricia Phagan, *Thomas Rowlandson. Pleasures and Pursuits in Georgian England*, Poughkeepsie, NY: The Frances Lehman Loeb Art Center, Vassar College, in association with London: D Giles, 2011

**Rodgers 1996**
David Rodgers, 'Rowlandson, Thomas (*b* London, 14 July 1756 or 1757; *d* London, 21 April 1827)', in Jane Turner (ed), *The Dictionary of Art*, London: Macmillan, 1996, Volume 27, pages 277-279

**Sabin 1933**
V P Sabin, *A Catalogue of Watercolour Drawings by Thomas Rowlandson (1756-1827)*, London: Frank T Sabin, 1933

**Wark 1975**
Robert Wark, *Drawings by Thomas Rowlandson*, San Marino, CA: Huntington Library, 1975


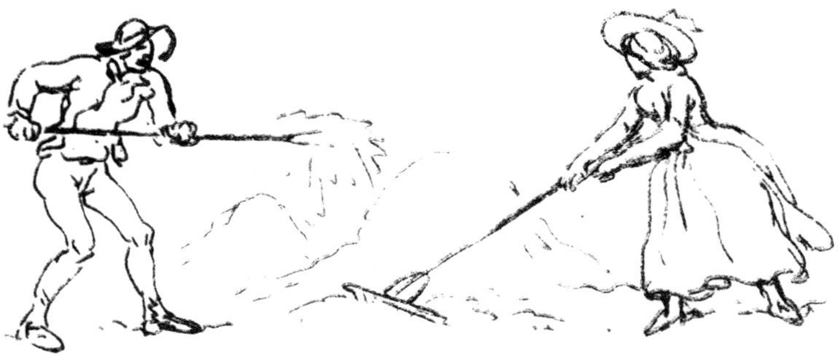

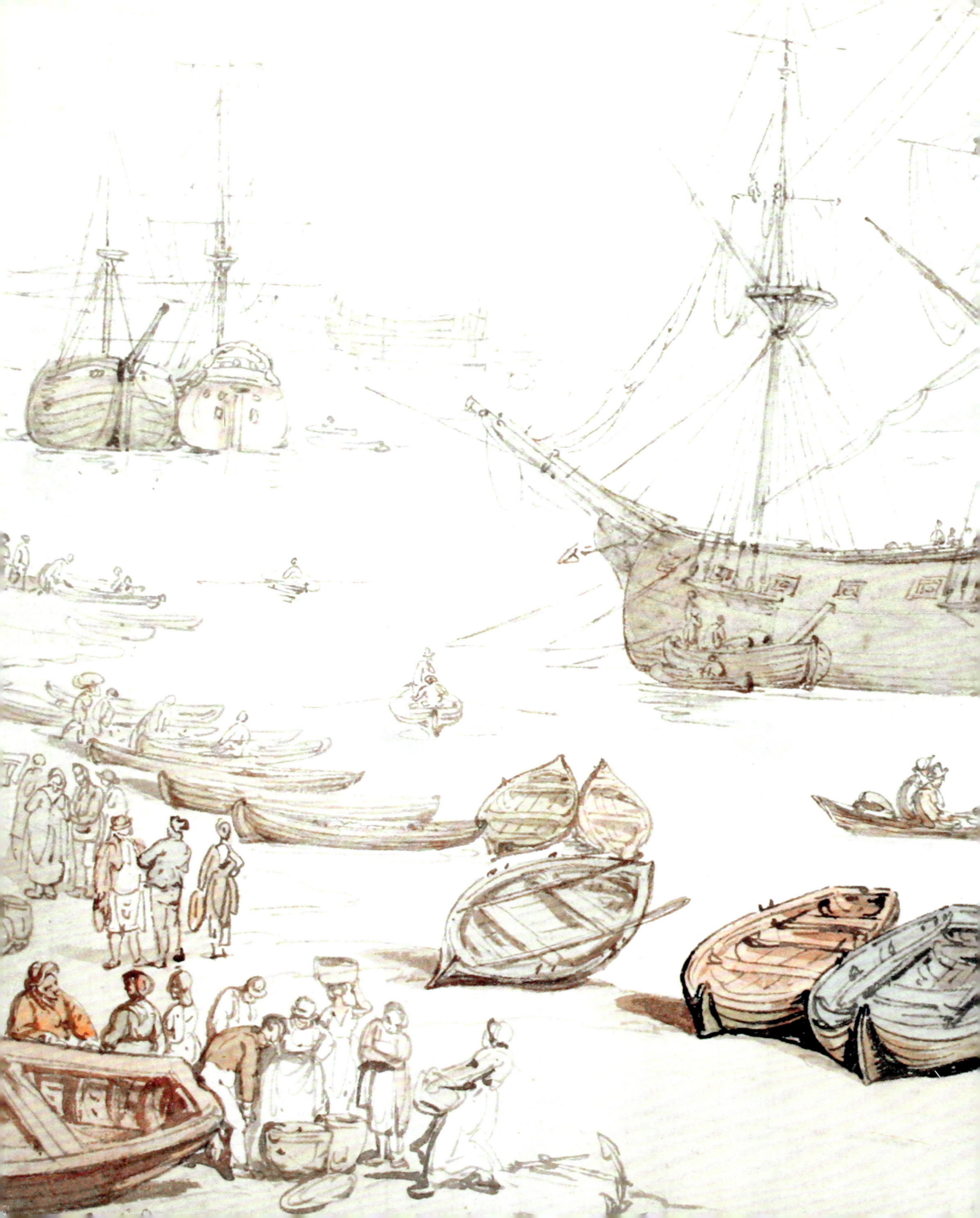